Don't Go There.

It's Not Safe.

You'll Die.

and other more rational advice for

OVERLANDING

Mexico & Central America

www.LifeRemotely.com

Written by Jared McCaffree, Jessica Mans & Kobus Mans

ISBN 978-0-9835127-4-5

www.LifeRemotely.com

Contents

Don't Go There.

It's Not Safe.

You'll Die.

We've received a huge variety of reactions from friends, family and strangers when they hear about our trip. "You're driving to *where*?!" Often followed by, "Are you bringing a gun?" and, "I heard they just found 14 more dead bodies in Mexico."

We met a guy in southern Mexico who was riding his motorcycle from the US to Panama. He was earnestly warned that Mexicans use dead babies to transport drugs across the border. "How could you possibly be safe in a country that does that?" To us, this stands as a testament to how screwed up people's perspectives can become.

Sensationalizing horrific stories is nothing new. It's easy to apply negative stereotypes to a country when you only hear the worst. Imagine if everything you knew about your hometown came from the local news. Would you want to go there?

Travel in Mexico and Central America is not without risk. Non-violent crimes such as petty theft, police corruption and traveler scams are real threats. And every country has areas that are best avoided, especially parts of the capitol. What you need to survive is common sense and practical knowledge, not a gun or bulletproof windows.

With very few exceptions, the people we've met on this trip have been helpful, hospitable and incredibly friendly. After spending 70 days and driving 4,500 miles in Mexico it's one of the countries we most want to return to.

So when people tell you not to go there, that it isn't safe, and that you'll die, take it with a grain of salt. Fear of your safety and of the unknown are not reasons to avoid travel in Latin America. Every country we've visited has been amazing and full of kind, welcoming people who certainly do not spend their free time stuffing drugs into dead bodies.

Introduction

What's This Book All About?

This is a book for people who want to travel by car in Mexico and Central America. The information contained within this book is a result of our eight-month overlanding trip from Seattle to Panama and the hundreds of hours of research we did before leaving home.

This book provides information on preparing for the trip and gives an idea of what to expect once you hit the road. We've also compiled specific information about each country we've visited. This includes border crossings, driving conditions, internet, cell phones, expenses, and a few awesome places we visited.

Although we have written specifically about Mexico and Central America, much of the information in the first two parts of this book can be applied to overlanding anywhere in the world.

We will expand this book to include South America after the completion of our trip in 2013.

Why Overland?

Traveling with your own vehicle gives you an incredible amount of flexibility. It also opens up opportunities that are difficult if not impossible to achieve by other forms of travel. You have the ability to change your itinerary at a moment's notice, go places far off the traditional tourist trail, and spend more time enjoying the wide open spaces between points A and B.

You aren't dependent on private taxis and tours. There is no need to decode the riddle of public transportation, or place your belongings and itinerary into someone else's hands. The freedom to go where you want, when you want, is yours.

Traveling in your own vehicle is also much more comfortable. With a bit of preparation you can have consistent and easy access to basic amenities such as hot food, cold drinks, a place to sleep, and even a shower. You have more freedom to bring gear without the worries of having to carry it on your back. A laptop, a stack of books, full-sized first-aid kit, propane stove, a proper mattress; it's a matter of cubic meters rather than liters.

It's easy to stop a car when you drive by something interesting. This is not the case for a tour bus or airplane. We have had many amazing experiences and met remarkable people simply by chance encounters while on our way to the next stop.

The freedom to go where you want, when you want, is yours.

It's Not All Fun and Games

Traveling by car certainly has its advantages, but there are several serious concerns that all overlanders must come to terms with. It is no simple matter to drive this distance, through every type of road condition imaginable, in countries where the rules of the road are treated more as suggestions than laws. At times it takes nerves of steel to get through the day unscathed.

One of the biggest concerns for overlanders is the reliability of their vehicle. Breaking down is never a fun experience. Being in a foreign country with a potential language barrier and limited replacement parts can make the situation much worse. All of your belongings rest on those wheels, and when they stop spinning, you go nowhere. It takes constant work to maintain your vehicle. The best tools to get you through tough times are a good knowledge of your vehicles' mechanics, coupled with a decent grasp of the Spanish language.

Keep in mind that there are bad people everywhere.

Safety is usually the number one cause of anxiety before heading out on this trip. Much can be done before you leave in terms of research and modifications to your vehicle, but once you hit the road a strong dose of common sense will help the most. Finding safe and secure areas to leave your car is an ongoing concern. It can be difficult and stressful at times, but we have always been able to find a place to park that allowed us to sleep well at night.

Keep in mind that there are bad people everywhere. Don't let media hype or paranoid friends and family dissuade you. Plenty of overlanders finish this trip each year, and aside from occasional petty crime, you will not hear many complaints.

The cost of gas is another consideration that needs to be factored into the trip. It's not cheap, but it's an expense that's easy to offset by exploiting the benefits of overlanding. The ability to camp, cook your own meals, and avoid paying other transportation costs more than makes up for the price at the pump. Also consider that if you did this trip over the course of a year and a half, you would probably drive less than the average American commuter.

As many road trippers will attest, the benefits of overlanding far outweigh the negatives. You certainly will have additional worries, expenses and logistics to deal with. In return you gain added comfort, the freedom to travel where you wish, and the ability to alter your schedule on a whim.

Who Are You People?

We are Life Remotely. Our goal is to sustain travel by working online. Our website combines travel information, advice for working while you travel, and a blog highlighting our trip from Seattle to Ushuaia. In October 2011 we left our home and started a 25,000-mile, 18-month road trip to the southern-most point in the Americas.

Life Remotely was created by Jessica Mans, Kobus Mans, and Jared McCaffree. We share a common passion of travel, and a lifestyle that permits us to spend our time where we choose. When we started our trip to Argentina we became digital nomads, combining our love for travel and the need to continue working.

Our hope is to provide useful information for others who wish to do the same, and in the process chronicle our journeys around the globe. Read more about our professional and travel backgrounds on our website, www.LifeRemotely.com.

Part 1:

PLANNING

1

Routes and Timelines

There are countless options for planning your route and timeline. We've met folks who have driven from Canada to Central America in less than two weeks, and a couple who began their journey in England and have been on the road for more than two years. One statement is universal amongst travelers: you will want to stay longer in nearly every place you go.

Setting a Timeline

A timeline of around one year seems to be the average when driving from the US or Canada to Argentina, with roughly half of the time spent in North and Central America, and the rest in South America. We plan to take 18 months for our drive from Seattle to Argentina, eight of which we spent in the US, Mexico and Central America.

We would not recommend attempting to drive the full distance to Argentina in under a year unless you really enjoy driving and don't mind skipping a lot of attractions. It certainly is possible; we recently met the guys from Adventuretheamericas.com who intend to drive from Colorado to Ushuaia and back in six months. For us it was more important to save more, spend less time driving and have the freedom to slow down and enjoy the sights. For them, it's all about driving, and arriving home in time for the Colorado ski season.

FOR MORE INFO SEARCH LIFEREMOTELY.COM

Creating a Travel Itinerary

Keep in mind the faster you travel the more you will spend on gas per day. Gas is a big part of the expense of this trip. Slowing down will not increase your expenses proportionally. Meaning that if you take double the time to complete this drive, you won't spend double the money on gas.

The Right Time of Year

Weather may play a part in deciding when you start the trip and how long you plan to be on the road. Avoiding the rainy season in Central America between mid-May and October is advisable, but not essential. There are places that become difficult to reach if rains are heavy, especially in Costa Rica. Rivers run high and poorly conditioned roads in remote areas are likely to wash out.

Winter in Alaska, northern Canada, and southern Chile and Argentina (Patagonia) is rough. The days are very short, snow can make it difficult to get around, and attractions may be closed. For this reason most people choose to enter Mexico between November and February and reach Patagonia 8 to 10 months later, in time for summer in the Southern Hemisphere. If you are on a shorter timeline, entering Mexico in spring or early summer is doable, however it will be very hot in lower elevations and you will hit the worst of the rainy season in Central America.

If you want to take a cruise to Antarctica from Argentina keep in mind that these only operate in the summer months, December to mid-March.

It helps to stay informed about local holidays, and know when high season is in full swing. Local holidays can be fun cultural experiences, or they can mean an entire city shuts down, making it hard to find a place to eat or sleep. High season brings increased prices in hotels and attractions, along with an influx of tourists that have a tendency to turn the best travel experiences into camera-dodging free-for-alls.

Any travel guidebook can give you high-season dates for specific areas, it's up to you to choose whether to steer clear or dive in. The biggest holidays in Latin America are usually part of the Catholic religion. But that doesn't mean they don't involve huge street parties with plenty of bootleg alcohol, illegal fireworks and music loud enough to disturb the dead.

Choosing a Route

Embarking on a Pan-American adventure is about more than just driving down the Pan-American Highway. At times we deviated from the main north/south highway by hundreds of miles. Other times it was the only road that could get us where we wanted to go.

The Pan-American starts in Prudhoe Bay, Alaska and ends in Ushuaia, Argentina. The only interruption is the Darien Gap, at the border of Panama and Colombia. Some people choose to begin their trip in northern Alaska for the sake of driving the entire distance of the Pan-American. Others start from wherever home is. Non-US residents commonly fly to Alaska or California to purchase a vehicle and start their journey.

Where you begin, and how much time you spend in the US and Canada is entirely your decision. We've met Canadians from half a dozen provinces, and Americans who hail from California to Massachusetts. Some spend months traveling across the States and Canada, visiting friends and family before crossing into Mexico. Others head directly to the border.

The Pan-American Highway is the world's longest "motorable road". measuring 29,800 miles (47,958 kilometers).

It's also possible to do the route in "backwards". In Panama we met overlanders from Argentina who are spending two years driving north to Alaska.

Planning a route between Mexico and Panama will force you to make four broad choices. Will you visit the Baja and Yucatan Peninsulas in Mexico, and do you want to go to the Central American countries of Belize and El Salvador? We hit all four, and even though it meant sacrificing time elsewhere, we have no regrets.

Our Route

Below is a breakdown of how much time we spent in each country between in the US and Panama:

Country	Days	Arrival Date
USA	28	10/8/11
Mexico	70	11/7/11
Belize	10	1/14/12
Guatemala	62	1/24/12
El Salvador	11	3/26/12
Honduras	3 hours	4/6/12
Nicaragua	14	4/6/12
Costa Rica	38	4/20/12
Panama	21	5/28/12
Total	**254**	

2

Keeping It Flexible

There isn't much point in coming up with anything but a rough itinerary for this trip. It's too long, and there are far too many unknowns. Having a rigid and detailed itinerary will lead only to unnecessary stress and disappointment.

Some people prefer to wing it every day. Others, like us, know just enough to have a rough idea when we are going to enter and leave each country. We do this so we can be sure to stay on budget and make it to Patagonia before the weather turns ugly. It helps to keep us from missing out on good stuff down the road, but also provides enough flexibility that we can stay a bit longer in places we enjoy.

Here are a few tips to keep your plans as flexible as possible while still maintaining a bit of sanity.

Stretch the Timeline

There is never enough time. Never. Even if you give yourself a year to travel, you will want more. The key is to stretch your schedule as much as possible. Add extra time that you can use up when you find a perfect place to hang out for a week.

Consider that you may reach a point where you need to stay in one place for a while. You can't hold a steady pace forever. Eventually your car will break down, you will get sick, have family visit, or just plain get tired of the road. You don't want to have to skip a country or go home early because you caught Guatemalan bird flu or your car needs a new transmission.

Do Your Homework

Before you start putting dates on a calendar, research and document where you want to go. If you're like us, you'll have a year or two to kill while you're saving money. Use this time to help reduce stress by coming up with ideas of places you'd like to go.

FOR MORE INFO SEARCH LIFEREMOTELY.COM

Researching Travel Destinations

How to Document Travel Destination Research

Highlight travel guides, talk to friends, and consult travel forums. Figure out what looks like fun and what you should avoid. Don't forget to watch for important events like festivals and holidays. They can be both awesome experiences and logistical nightmares.

Make a list of what you'd like to see and do and how much time you'd need to do it. Be realistic, seek more than one source of information, and consult with people who have recently done the same.

Get a Map

Once you have a list of places it's time to play a gigantic game of connect the dots. Plot out your top priority stops on a map to get a sense of how far apart they are. It was easy for us to rule out several places we wanted to visit simply because they were so far out of the way. The goal of this exercise isn't to come up with a specific route. It's to get an idea of which countries and regions interest you the most.

Having a rough idea will help you make a good decision once you're closer to the destination and are able to take into account variables that you can't predict while sitting at home. Tired of the heat? Want to spend time on the beach? Is the cost of gas eating a hole in your wallet? Is the road flooded? The point of not over-planning is to let these factors guide you when you're trying to figure out where next to go.

It may also help to discover what it logistically takes to get between destinations. For example: ferries, road conditions, road closures and paperwork like park permits. A bit of research into the cost of taking the Baja Peninsula ferry, or your ability to drive the Osa Peninsula in Costa Rica during the rainy season may help you rule out certain excursions early on.

FOR MORE INFO SEARCH LIFEREMOTELY.COM

Plan Your Trip with Google Earth and Google Maps

We prefer paper maps for planning and discussions, but Google Maps works best to get an estimate of the distance and time it will take to drive a stretch of road. Keep in mind that the route it chooses may not be the best, and you should always add 25-50% to the estimated driving time for all roads in Central America. Google's not great at accounting for flooded rivers, road construction, speed bumps or stray herds of cows.

You can also save your Google Map routes for later, and open them with Google Earth to build a full route map. We used Google Earth to map out a rough route, and continually update it as we travel.

Add Extra Drive Time

In the US and Canada a 400-mile day is doable, anywhere south of the Mexican border, not a chance. It will take more time and energy to get where you need to go than you are used to. A 150-mile, 6-hour day is not unheard of. Unless you enjoy endurance driving, or have a team of people to swap places at the wheel, you're going to have a much better time if you average less time on the road per day.

It's very common to have an hour or two added to your drive time by unexpected circumstances. We go out of our way to avoid turning a long day into a very long day. For starters, we avoid driving more than six hours each day. The idea is to not spend all day in the car, or worse, arriving at our next stop in the dark. We also try to avoid back-to-back driving days of more than four hours. This helps to keep us from killing each other.

Don't Be Scared of Days Off

The days in between are for doing laundry, cleaning out the truck, updating the blog, going on a tour, taking a nap or just relaxing on the beach with a cold frosty beverage. You don't have to go anywhere, but you can if you want. In a good week, we have at least three days off.

> Don't be scared of having days without plans, they will often be the best days.

We don't really plan our free days ahead of time, they happen as a result of a flexible schedule. If we're bored, we go do something. If we're tired, we lay around in hammocks. Don't be scared of having days without plans, they will often be the best days.

3

Budget & Money

For most of us, the amount of time we have to travel is directly proportional to the amount of money in our bank account. Stretching your cash means stretching the amount of time you can spend on the road.

FOR MORE INFO SEARCH LIFEREMOTELY.COM

Introduction to Travel Budgeting

What to Consider before Creating a Travel Budget

Coming up with a budget and sticking to it is an inconvenience. We make the effort because we want to finish this trip before the money runs out, or even better, continue traveling. Knowing how much we have to spend helps us decide what to do on a daily basis. If we're under budget we'll splurge for tours or nights out on the town. If we're over budget we know to stock up on rice and beans at the next grocery store.

Budgeting is like planning an itinerary: it doesn't do any good if it isn't flexible. However, the more flexible your itinerary is, the more haphazard your budget will be. If you care about the bottom line, and you want to keep a flexible schedule, it will mean more time spent adjusting your budget and crunching numbers. There is no easy fix for this, you have to find a middle ground that works for you, and that may involve spending time tabbing through spreadsheets while sipping a margarita on the beach.

Getting an Idea of the Cost

The question of how much you should save in order to start this trip is not easily answered. What you spend before heading out the door is a product of your personal preferences and what you own before the trip starts. It's possible to start this trip without spending a dime. Others choose to spend years and tens of thousands of dollars outfitting their vehicle.

How much you spend each day while you travel largely depends on where you sleep and how cheaply you can eat. Camping for free and eating rice, beans and fresh produce will get you through the day for practically nothing but the cost of gas. If you can sleep in your vehicle, it's easy to find free or at least cheap places to park for the night. Staple food prices between Mexico and Panama are very low, with the exception of Costa Rica. Cooking meals for yourself can cost just a couple dollars per day.

The more you camp and cook for yourself, the more you will save.

Paying for hotel rooms and eating meals out will considerably increase your daily costs. Food and lodging prices become cheaper the farther south you go, again with the exception of Costa Rica and parts of Panama. However, there is still a big difference between paying $25 for a hotel room and $5 for a place to camp. The more you camp and cook for yourself, the more you will save.

It's also important to factor in the cost of activities. Tours, park fees and other forms of entertainment can be huge expenses relative to food and lodging. It's nearly impossible to budget for each activity. We found it best to just add a set amount of money (for us, $14 per day) to our budget that acts as a buffer. If all goes according to plan, we end up under budget and can spend more money on entertainment. If we're over budget, we tend to do fewer activities.

A Quick Glance at Our Total Costs

We fall somewhere in the middle when it comes to our expenses. We tent camp roughly two thirds of our nights, and rarely spend a night for free. We cook our own food most of the time, but we eat well, buying meat for almost every meal and drinks for when the sun goes down.

FOR MORE INFO SEARCH LIFEREMOTELY.COM

How Much Will All This Cost?

Budget Recaps Per Country

Below is a breakdown of what the three of us spent before we left home, and how much the 254 days and 13,000 miles between Seattle and Panama cost us.

Startup Costs		**Trip Costs**	
Vehicle	$7,500	Food	$7,500
Vehicle Maintenance & Mods	$4,500	Lodging	$5,100
Gear	$1,000	Gas	$3,000
Insurance	$2,000	Other*	$7,400
Total	$15,000	Total	$23,000

* Includes: border crossings, supplies, vehicle maintenance, entertainment, laundry, drinks, park fees, tolls, phone, internet, gifts, six weeks of Spanish school, and other transportation costs.

What it Cost Other Overlanders

While startup costs vary widely, it seems that most Pan-American duos manage to spend under $70 per day. These folks commonly chose a 12 to 18 month timeframe to drive the entire Pan-American and plan to camp and buy most food from grocery stores. We've met people who move at a snail's pace and spend less than $25 per day. And others on such a short timeframe that gas costs them more than $30 per day.

On average, overlanding couples spend $70 per day.

Below are links to spending reports published by friends we've met on the road and other overlanders who have recently finished the trip.

Brianna and Logan of PanAmNotes.com spent 449 days on the road between their home in San Francisco and Ushuaia, Argentina. Their website includes a detailed breakdown of their expenses and budget, and costs by country. The couple spent nearly $23,000 on startup costs, and budgeted $11,000 for one-time expenses such as shipping their car across the Darien and paying for visas and insurance. On average they spent $72 per day on gas, food, lodging, drinks, tours and entertainment.

Dan of TheRoadChoseMe.com spent 22 months on his 50,000-mile trek across the Americas. At the end of his trip he posted about his expenses on his blog. He reports that his trip cost a total of $27,300 including $7,000 for gas and $3,500 for big expenses like flights, ferries, tours and shipping his Jeep across the Darien Gap. His startup costs were limited to his Jeep, which he purchased for $6,250 and sold for $5,000 when the trip was finished.

Kristin and Chris of TheDarienPlan.com spent 16 months driving from their home in California to Argentina. They are cofounders of one of the best resources for overlanding in North and South America, DriveTheAmericas.com. Their travel blog includes a financial wrap-up of their trip with a breakdown of what they spent on insurance, flights, ferries and shipping around the Darien Gap. It also includes a cost breakdown by country, which averaged $71 per day for the two of them.

Our road tripping friends James and Lauren of HomeontheHighway.com publish monthly summaries of expenses on their blogs. And our website contains budget recaps of what we've spent in each country.

Estimating Your Expenses

Figuring out how much money you will need goes hand-in-hand with researching where you want to go. As you look through guidebooks and search the internet, write down average costs of hotel rooms, campgrounds, park fees, gas, meals...anything that you can use to get a rough idea of what your expenses may be.

Calculating the cost of gas is a matter of using Google Maps or a paper map to figure out roughly how many miles you will drive in each country. Given the estimated price of gas per country, and your car's fuel efficency, you can calculate the total amount you will spend on gas.

We played it safe and lowered our fuel efficiency by 25% to give us an added buffer in case we drove more, gas prices went up, or road conditions were worse than expected. This helped us immensely when we realized the price of gas had risen $1 per gallon in Central America since we had done our research.

To calculate lodging costs, use a sampling of prices for hotels and campgrounds from websites and guidebooks. Looking at other overlanders budgets is also very helpful. We conservatively planned to camp 50% of our nights once we left the US, and adjusted our average accordingly.

As a good rule of thumb, cheap hotels from Mexico to Panama average $25

High-octane gas cost us an average of $4.77 per gallon.

for a double, hostels are $10 per person, and campgrounds are $5 per person. Prices vary widely depending on how urban and touristy an area is. Be aware that prices in guidebooks will probably be lower than what you end up paying. Once Lonely Planet sticks their star of approval on a place, prices will go up.

Food costs depend on what you eat and how many meals you eat out. Our plan was $8 per person, per day outside of the US. In reality it was closer to $10, even though we eat less than one in ten meals in a restaurant. If you're vegetarian or if you can get by with rice, beans, tortillas, fresh produce and the occasional leg of chicken, your expenses will be lower.

How We Budget: The Short(er) Version

Step 1: Make a Budget

Our budget is different for each country. We include the number of days we want to spend in each country, with estimates of lodging, food and gas prices. To that we added a fixed amount to cover miscellaneous expenses such as tours, supplies and fees for internet and phone use. This gives our daily budget a bit of flexibility. Add it all up and you have our per diem, how much we expect to spend each day, per country.

FOR MORE INFO SEARCH LIFEREMOTELY.COM

How to Create a Travel Budget

Sample Travel Budget

Country	Days	Arrival	Food	Camping	Hotel	%Camp	Total
USA	30	10/8/2011	$40.00	$20.00	$100.00	80%	$2,280.00
Mexico	68	11/7/2011	$25.00	$15.00	$25.00	50%	$3,060.00
Belize	10	1/14/2012	$30.00	$15.00	$30.00	50%	$525.00
Guatemala	7	1/24/2012	$20.00	$10.00	$15.00	50%	$227.50
Guate Volunteer	55	1/31/2012	$35.00	$0.00	$35.00	0%	$3,850.00
Honduras	0	3/26/2012	$25.00	$10.00	$20.00	50%	$0.00
El Salvador	11	3/26/2012	$25.00	$15.00	$35.00	50%	$550.00
Nicaragua	14	4/6/2012	$25.00	$15.00	$30.00	50%	$665.00
Costa Rica	38	4/20/2012	$25.00	$15.00	$25.00	50%	$1,710.00
Panama	21	5/28/2012	$25.00	$15.00	$25.00	50%	$945.00
Colombia	28	6/18/2012	$25.00	$10.00	$15.00	50%	$1,050.00
Ecuador	21	7/16/2012	$25.00	$10.00	$15.00	50%	$787.50
Peru	45	8/6/2012	$25.00	$10.00	$25.00	50%	$1,912.50
Bolivia	21	9/20/2012	$25.00	$5.00	$10.00	50%	$682.50
Chile	60	10/11/2012	$25.00	$15.00	$25.00	50%	$2,700.00
Argentina	60	12/10/2012	$25.00	$15.00	$30.00	50%	$2,850.00

We also made a list of one-time expenses per country. Visas, vehicle import costs, tours and boat trips top the list. Visas and vehicle import costs are not extreme between the US and Panama, but taking the ferry from La Paz to Mazatlan will cost at least $300 USD.

One-Time Costs Per Person

Machu Picchu Hike	$450.00
Flight Home	$600.00
Antarctica	$4,500.00
Shipping Car Darien	$400.00
Flights to Cartagena	$300.00
Ferry to Baja	$133.33
Car Insurance 1mo	$50.00
Mexico Border	$15.00
Honduras Border	$13.33
Guatemala Border	$3.33
Belize Exit Fee	$13.33
Nicaragua Border	$6.67
Costa Rica Border	$4.00
Panama Border	$4.00
Colombia Border	$15.00
Vehicle Maintenance	$500.00
Total	**$7,008.00**

Also included in our budget are startup costs: our car, maintenance and modifications, gear, immunizations and everything else we spent before leaving home. The closer we got to our departure date, the more this list grew.

To round out the budget we included $10 per person, per day of "spending money". Beer and cigarette money, if you will. Because there are three of us, and only two of us are financially entangled, we spend our own money on personal expenses. Stuff like souvenirs, liquor, medicine and chocolate bars.

We don't track personal expenses, so it's not included in the breakdowns in this book. However, we can say with certainty that we haven't come close to spending $10 per person, per day on personal expenses. This money was put aside to buffer our trip expenses as much as it was to buy souvenirs. If our per diem costs run over, the money comes from the same place - our personal bank accounts.

And finally, the budget includes $1,500 of "emergency" money. This is to cover car repairs, and to give us a supply of cash to keep on hand in case we run into unexpected problems. Having this money set aside helps keep us sane if something bad happens.

Step 2: Follow the Budget

FOR MORE INFO SEARCH LIFEREMOTELY.COM

Financial Planning for Travel Emergencies

The best way we've found to stick to our budget on the road is to have a bank account specifically for the purpose of the trip. Money is transferred into that account periodically, roughly every two to three months, and we use that account for all cash withdraws.

Account Balance	1209.84
Emergency Money	659.60
Cash on Hand	84.63
Adjusted Balance	634.87
Expected Balance	1525.36
Difference	-890.49

To make balancing the budget easy, we created a spreadsheet listing the expected balance of our travel bank account each day. Given our per diem expenses (food, gas, lodging & supplies) plus our one-time expenses (tours, border crossings and big transportation costs) we can figure out what the bank account balance should be on any given day.

Budget Balancing 101

1. Get your bank account balance.
2. Subtract any money in your bank account that's for emergency use only.
3. Add any cash you have on hand. This is your adjusted balance.
4. Check your handy per diem spreadsheet; find the row with today's date. This is your expected balance.
5. Subtract #3 from #4.
6. If it's positive, buy more beer! If it's negative, you're over budget.

FOR MORE INFO SEARCH LIFEREMOTELY.COM

How to use a Travel Budget on the Road

You may also want to track individual expenses to get an idea where your money is going. We use a good old-fashioned pen and paper to accomplish this. Each time money comes out of the wallet we list the cost and category: gas, camping, hotels, groceries, eating out, supplies, etc. We periodically total the numbers in a spreadsheet to get an idea of our expense breakdown.

We go to great detail tracking our expenses, mainly because we have the manpower and the desire to publish the data on our webpage for the benefit of others. In the end our expense tracking tells us more about the actual costs of a country after the fact, rather than providing ways to save money en route. Occasionally it shows us how our original budget was wrong, which helps when making revisions down the road.

Step 3: Update the Budget

Our budget is based on expected expenses per day, multiplied by the number of days we plan to spend in that country. However, we've never crossed a border on the date we originally expected. Lesson learned: if you want to carefully watch your finances and have a flexible itinerary, you have to spend time maintaining your budget while traveling.

We update our budget roughly every two months. The idea is to zero-out our travel bank account and start from scratch. This means that we recalculate our per diem expenses, update the amounts we expect to spend in the future, and transfer money into our travel account to cover the next stretch of the trip.

There's no myth or mystery to this process, just a bit of calculator and spreadsheet work. If we are over budget, we transfer more money to cover the next leg of the trip. If we're under, we transfer less. What matters is that we revisit our budget, put things back on track, and pick up the pieces after a month spent drinking too many $10 bottles of rum in Costa Rica.

Our Expenses

The bottom line: it cost us about $38,000 for our eight-month drive to Panama, or $12,667 per person. Our total 18-month trip to Argentina is expected to cost $70,000, which breaks down to $23,333 per person, or $1,300 per person, per month.

FOR MORE INFO SEARCH LIFEREMOTELY.COM

How Much Will All This Cost?

It cost us $15,000 to get out the door. Half of that was spent buying our 4Runner, and the rest on vehicle maintenance, modifications, gear, and insurance. The cost of getting started was roughly 40% of the total cost of the trip to Panama.

We have an average of $80 per day, $27 per person, budgeted for per diem expenses like food, gas, lodging, entertainment, and supplies. Once you factor in border crossings, car repairs and big expenses like the Baja ferry, we spent an average of $90 per day.

On top of our per diem expenses, we have $6,000 per person set aside for known one-time expenses for our entire trip to Argentina. This includes border crossing costs, big transportation expenses like the Baja ferry and shipping our car across the Darien Gap. Of this $6,000 budgeted we spent $2,500 between Mexico and Panama, $1,950 of which was the cost to get our car and ourselves to Colombia. The rest of our one-time budget is reserved for a few big tours in South America including a cruise to Antarctica and hiking the Inca Trail in Peru.

Detailed Startup Costs

Vehicle		Gear	
'97 Toyota 4Runner	$7,600.00	Phone, 3G Modem & Router	$325.00
Dual Battery System	$943.00	Guidebooks	$200.00
New Tires	$620.00	GPS	$200.00
Replacement Parts	$605.00	Paper Maps	$180.00
Vehicle Maintenance	$580.00	Water Purifier	$65.00
Tools & Hi-Lift Jack	$465.00	**Total Gear**	**$970.00**
Refrigerator	$425.00		
Security System	$415.00	**Car Insurance**	
Storage Modifications	$240.00	Central & South America	$1,848.00
Stereo System	$175.00	Mexico	$184.00
Total Vehicle	**$12,068.00**	**Total Car Ins**	**$2,032.00**

Total Startup Costs	**$15,070.00**

One-Time Expenses Per Country

These expenses include the cost to take the Baja ferry from La Paz to Mazatlan and shipping our car and flying from Panama to Colombia, excluding Colombian port fees. It also includes costs at borders such as visas, vehicle import permits, fumigation and mandatory insurance.

USA	$0.00
Mexico	$390.00
Belize	$28.00
Guatemala	$24.00
El Salvador	$0.00
Nicaragua	$72.00
Costa Rica	$36.00
Panama	$1,950.00
Total	**$2,500.00**

Expense Breakdown Per Country

Do you want to know the nitty-gritty details? Here they are. The chart below is a breakdown of what we spent in every country for all of the categories of expenses we track. For more detailed insights on each country, see Part 3.

	USA	Mexico	Belize	Guatemala	El Salvador	Nicaragua	Costa Rica	Panama	Total
Total Days	28	70	10	62	11	14	38	19	252
Lodging	$839	$1,209	$176	$1,371	$259	$209	$451	$624	$5,140
Groceries	$488	$1,155	$152	$436	$186	$255	$854	$314	$3,843
Eating Out	$653	$936	$246	$1,291	$69	$187	$160	$119	$3,663
Gas	$744	$743	$25	$494	$99	$198	$404	$278	$2,988
Entertainment	$21	$54	$0	$1,954	$80	$42	$98	$75	$2,326
Supplies	$276	$102	$4	$259	$9	$74	$58	$158	$943
Drinks	$259	$336	$58	$111	$13	$30	$41	$0	$850
Transport	$12	$335	$180	$206	$0	$67	$0	$32	$832
Park Fees	$110	$161	$45	$141	$10	$0	$144	$15	$627
Vehicle	$54	$0	$0	$356	$0	$0	$0	$0	$410
Internet & Phone	$17	$133	$0	$78	$0	$9	$20	$10	$267
Tolls & Parking	$21	$176	$7	$25	$1	$0	$21	$10	$263
Border Crossing	$0	$55	$28	$23	$0	$72	$36	$0	$215
Laundry	$19	$37	$10	$50	$16	$15	$33	$31	$213
Gifts	$0	$30	$0	$0	$0	$12	$9	$0	$52

Average Daily Expenses Per Country

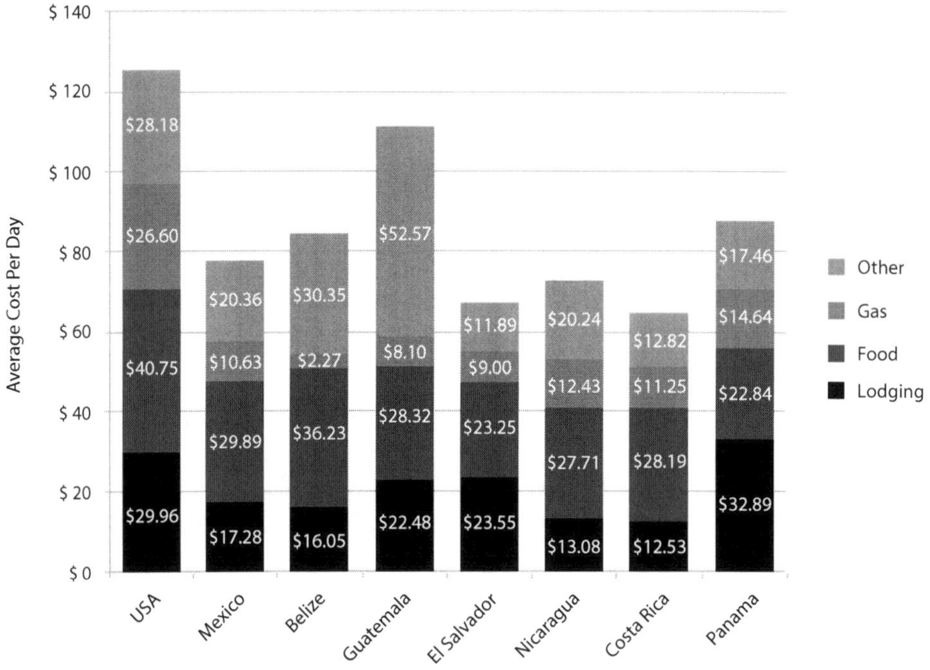

Note: In Guatemala our "other" expenses include six weeks of language school at a total cost of $1,875. The food and lodging categories each include $800 for the costs of our homestay program that covered lodging and meals six days a week.

Average Daily Lodging Costs Per Country

On average we spent $25.68 per night on accommodation and camped 63% of the time. The average hotel cost was $34 and the average cost to camp was $16 for three people.

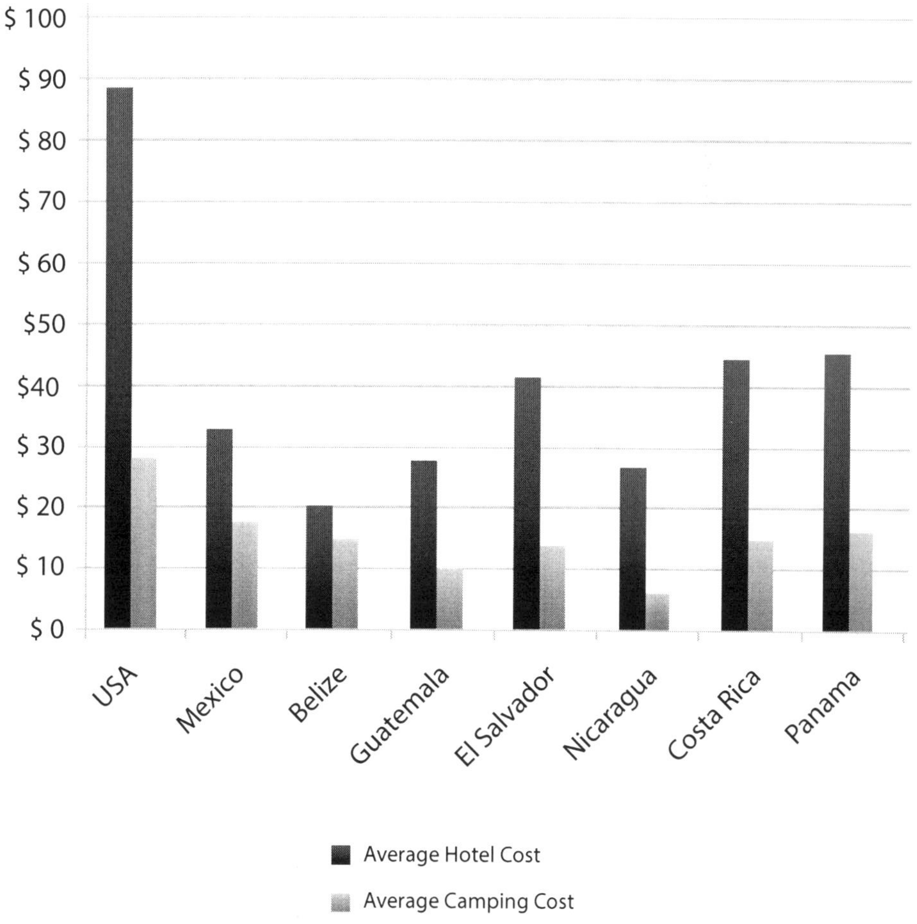

Breakdown of Gas Expenses Per Country

We spent a total of $3,077.78 on gas for our car, plus a couple fill-ups for a Costa Rican rental car. We used only premium gas because the price difference was negligible in Mexico and Central America. The average cost of a gallon was $4.77. Surpassing our expectations, the 4Runner averaged 17.5 miles per gallon over 13,000 miles.

	Total Spent	Miles	$/Gallon	MPG
USA	$744.73	3720	$3.93	19
Mexico	$743.86	4454	$2.98	18
Belize	$25.50	210	$5.90	17
Guatemala	$494.06	1489	$4.92	17
El Salvador	$270.00	439	$4.89	16
Nicaragua	$198.93	667	$5.47	18.5
Costa Rica	$322.45	983	$5.66	16
Panama	$278.25	1091	$4.40	18.5

Tips for Saving Money

Food

- Eating out is very expensive. One meal out easily buys us a couple days of groceries.
- Watch out for imported food. Prices will be equal to or more than you are used to paying at home. Learn to eat what the locals eat.
- If you want to eat out, roadside stands, markets, and small restaurants with fixed menus are the cheapest.

- If you are outside the US, El Salvador or Panama, and the menu lists prices in US dollars, walk away.
- Before crossing into more expensive countries (Belize, Costa Rica, and Panama) stock up on basic food items.
- Shopping at the local butcher, produce stand and bakery is the cheapest way to stock up on food. Central markets and small businesses are less convenient, but will always be cheaper than a supermarket.

Lodging

- Research campgrounds ahead of time. Look online and ask other travelers. Guidebooks are fairly useless for campground information. If you roll up to a town expecting to find a campground, you may end up staying in an expensive hotel.
- Finding places to sleep for free is the best way to save money. Restaurants, hotel parking lots, gas stations and beaches are your best bet.
- The more amenities a campground has, the more expensive it will be. Full-service RV parks in the US are a great example.
- Campground prices vary widely in Latin America. Sometimes you are charged per vehicle, the number of tents, or most commonly, per person.
- If you can't camp, try to find a hotel or hostel where you can cook. For us, it usually costs more to eat dinner in a restaurant than it does for a night in a cheap hotel.
- Rooms with AC are at least 25% more expensive. Often hotels have cheaper non-AC rooms but may not tell you unless you ask.

Driving

- The longer your trip, the less you will spend on gas each day. Consecutive driving days are a sure way to go over budget in the short term.
- Toll roads in Mexico can be expensive; we spent over $150 crossing the country. For us it was still better than the alternative, which was twice the driving time, plus added wear and tear on our vehicle.
- Gas prices went up nearly $1 per gallon since we researched this trip. Your best bet is to ask people in the countries ahead of you for up-to-date numbers. Gas prices don't significantly vary across a single country. In some countries such as Mexico and Costa Rica, gas prices are federally regulated and are the same at every gas station.
- Have an emergency fund for vehicle maintenance. It's peace of mind you will need when things go wrong.
- Keep a stack of cash hidden inside your vehicle in case the ATM machines go down or you run out of money at a border crossing.
- Consider taking public transportation. If you are staying in the same area for a while, and have a safe place to park your car, it may be a cheaper and more convenient way to take a side trip.

Internet

- Free wifi in cafés and restaurants is not free; you are obligated to buy a drink or food. But once you have the password, there's no harm in parking out front.
- Look for recognizable places that routinely have free internet. McDonalds, Starbucks, libraries, etc.

- If you need to spend a day on the internet, a campground with wifi is the cheapest option but the most difficult to find.
- Internet is very common and cheap throughout Mexico and Central America. Access is frequently found in hotels, hostels, restaurants and internet cafés in any decent-sized town.
- If you want to have internet almost everywhere, buy an unlocked multi-band 3G USB modem before you leave, and buy cheap prepaid SIM cards in each country you visit.

4

Choosing the Right Vehicle

During our eight months on the road to Panama we've met dozens of travelers following the Pan-American route, using every type of transportation imaginable. From ultra-lite backpacks to bicycles to a refurbished European fire engine from the 50s. There is no limit to the ways people choose to travel between North and South America.

Any vehicle sold could make this trip, given enough time and money. Your choice depends on your preferences, budget, mechanical aptitude, and where you want to go. Road conditions from Mexico to Panama are not great, but they are easily drivable if you stick to major highways and proceed carefully. A 4x4 and high ground clearance aren't required, although the lack of either will limit where you can go.

FOR MORE INFO SEARCH LIFEREMOTELY.COM

Choosing an Overland Vehicle

Common Choices

The most common choice of vehicle is a mid to full-sized SUV, truck, or van. Volkswagen vans, Toyota SUVs, and older Land Cruisers top the list. We've also seen larger vans and RVs, but rarely south of Mexico. Overlanders tend to choose the smallest car or truck that will fit their needs and budget. Driving a large vehicle is more difficult on cramped roads, not to mention much less fuel-efficient.

We know of people who have driven four-door sedans and even two-door hatchbacks, although we haven't met any on the road. Kelsey and Tom of Joydrive.ca, cofounders of DrivetheAmericas.com, completed their trip in December 2009 driving a '91 Volkswagen Golf over 31,000 miles without so much as a flat tire.

The common theme amongst overlanders is to be as self-sufficient as possible. Pack cooking gear and have a place to sleep that doesn't require a hotel reservation. Not only is this the best way to save money, it gives you the greatest flexibility when choosing where you want to go. You have the ability to spend more time off the grid, exploring remote locations without the worry of finding hotels and restaurants. It also allows you to stay in expensive touristy areas without breaking the bank.

The common theme amongst overlanders is to be as self-sufficient as possible.

Sleeping Space

If you are in the market for a vehicle specifically for this trip, first decide how you want to spend your nights. This will limit your choices more than any other decision. If you already have a vehicle, deciding where to spend your nights a matter of weighing the options. Your vehicle either includes a place to sleep or can be modified to include one. If sleeping inside your vehicle isn't an option, your choices are to tent camp or stay in hotels and hostels.

Sleeping Inside Your Vehicle

Having a bed inside your car is by far the most popular choice of sleeping arrangements. This can be accomplished by purchasing an SUV, pickup, van, or RV. Modifications most commonly consist of installing a rooftop tent or building a platform in the back of your vehicle to sleep on.

There are plenty of exceptions; we've seen restored Unimogs, European fire engines and converted trucks with ample living space. However, in most cases these are projects of a price and magnitude equal to or greater than the undertaking of this trip. Many of these folks go on to conquer more than just the Americas.

The two big benefits of sleeping inside your car are additional security and being able to camp for free in many locations. With proper preparation it can also be the most comfortable option, provided you have decent ventilation and protection from biting insects.

The cost of buying or outfitting a vehicle with an area for sleeping is the biggest downside. Every option, aside from simply mounting of a piece of plywood in the bed of a truck, will considerably increase how much money you need to get the show on the road. Having enough room for a bed may also be a problem. Storage space is incredibly valuable; much thought should go into justifying everything you take with you.

Rooftop tents are also a popular choice for people who want to avoid sleeping on the ground and either do not want to drive, or cannot afford to buy a larger vehicle. They can be easily installed on most any vehicle with a roof rack large enough to accommodate the tent. Prices for quality tents range from $1,000 to $5,000 or more.

Tent Camping

If you're OK with tent camping or spending your nights in hotels you can get by with just about any type of vehicle that has enough storage space for your gear.

We chose to tent camp largely because there are three of us. Buying, outfitting and driving a vehicle large enough to sleep everyone was prohibitively expensive. We also enjoy tent camping, and already had most of the necessary gear.

Space becomes less of an issue if you choose to tent camp. You are more exposed to nature, which is generally a good thing if you enjoy the outdoors and have a waterproof tent. Ventilation and bugs are less of an issue. It is very comforting to know you have a space you can sleep beyond the reach of biting insects.

The downside is that facilities for tent camping can be rare in some Central American countries. It's not as easy to find free camping areas, locating a place to park and pitch a tent can be difficult if your goal is to sleep unnoticed. Security is also a valid concern. For these reasons we rarely spend a night in our tents outside of a legitimate campground and we never leave anything valuable in our tents.

We've managed to camp roughly two thirds of our nights since leaving home. At times it is difficult to find camping facilities, especially in big cities. However, it is possible to drive from Alaska to Panama and spend nearly every night in a tent. When we stay in a hotel it's usually by choice. After spending a week or two in a tent the need for a hot shower, a proper mattress, and a fast internet connection win out over our wallet.

Living and Cooking Space

For a comfortable living area inside your vehicle you'll want to look at Volkswagen vans, full-sized vans like the Chevy Astro Van, smaller RVs, tow-behind trailers, or a camper on the back of a pickup. More creative options abound, but usually involve a significant investment of money and time.

> Packing a kitchen and being able to cook your own meals is one of the best ways to save money on a long road trip.

Sleeping on the bed of a pickup truck or SUV with the rear seats removed seems to be the most common choice for budget-minded overlanders who want to stay off the ground. This option doesn't leave room for much other living space. You're still stuck with cooking, eating and relaxing outside.

Shannon of RuinedAdventures.com and their modified Toyota 4Runner.

A more popular option is to have a semi-portable kitchen that can easily be setup next to your vehicle. Many overlanders cook on their tailgates, or have tables that easily extend from their cars. You can combine an external cooking area with an awning or mosquito-netted shelter. This provides protection from the elements and a large area to prepare meals.

As tent campers with no awning or internal cooking area, our living and cooking space is always somewhere between our car and tents. We pack chairs, a table, a bin of kitchen supplies and setup wherever we want to cook. It's a pain to lug around so much stuff, but it also means we can setup our kitchen anywhere we want, including hotel rooms. We also didn't have to spend any money on vehicle modifications and only needed to a buy a minimal amount of gear to complete the setup.

Maintenance and Fuel Efficiency

If you are buying a vehicle specifically for this trip, the cost of maintenance, and the availability of spare parts and trained mechanics should be a top concern. Unless you know all the ins-and-outs of your vehicle, and are comfortable doing most of your own repairs, choosing a vehicle common to Central America is a very good idea. No matter what you drive, you will eventually have a problem and need someone to help you.

We highly recommend driving a car that can be repaired in every country.

Having an idea of where your car is sold and serviced will give you an idea of its availability and the likelihood of finding parts and mechanics familiar with the vehicle. Check with the manufacturer of the vehicle and ask for locations of authorized service centers in the countries you plan to visit. Online research, especially on forums specific to your vehicle, will also shed some light on your chances of finding repairs south of the US border. Toyota's Global Website has been particularly useful for us.

Don't forget to include fuel efficiency when figuring out how much you have to spend on a vehicle. If you're planning to drive 25,000 miles from North America to Argentina, the difference between 20 miles per gallon and 15 miles per gallon is nearly $1,875 at $4.50 per gallon. And the difference between 20 miles per gallon and 10 is $5,625, about the cost of a used 4x4 in decent shape.

Off-Road Capabilities

If you want to go way off the beaten track, a 4x4 is a must. Even some of the more popular sights in Central America require a 4x4 to access, especially in the rainy reason. Side roads can quickly turn to gravel, and we've been on plenty of paved highways that rapidly deteriorated due to neglect, road construction, or landslides.

Some overlanders choose a 4x4 because they actively seek off-road conditions as part of their trip experience. We don't do much off-roading "for fun"; it's more of a necessity to get to where we want to go. Our 4x4 has come in handy quite a few times, often unexpectedly. It has taken us to some spectacular places we would have otherwise missed.

The Border Runner of RuinedAdventures.com on the dirt roads of Ecuador.

It is helpful to have higher than average clearance when driving on highways due to unseen potholes, speed bumps, rocks, and missing manhole covers. However, if you drive carefully it's not necessary. If you plan to actively seek out off-road terrain, the more clearance you have the better. Many off-road trails are little more than washed out riverbeds strewn with differential-shattering boulders.

FOR MORE INFO SEARCH LIFEREMOTELY.COM

Why You Need 4x4 Driving Training

Another consideration is waterproofing. Off-roading in Central America will likely require that you cross a river or six. Know how deep you can go, and read up on what it takes to make your engine, transmission, axles, and electrical components waterproof. There is an excellent write up on how to protect your vehicle at CentralOverland.com.

5

Finding and Buying Your Vehicle

Choosing the right vehicle is only half the battle. Once you've narrowed down the field it's a matter of finding the right car. This can take much longer and involve quite a few more hassles, especially if you're on a tight budget and looking for a used car.

We knew exactly what we wanted and were willing to pay and it took us four months to find our 4Runner. We traveled 500 miles to pick him up. On the way we had a flat tire, drove through a torrential rainstorm, and one of us spent most of the trip puking in the back seat. It was a good practice run.

Finding Your Vehicle

Come up with a routine. If you want to get the best price and a vehicle in good condition it will take time. We perused the classified ads every day looking for possibilities. Craigslist was especially helpful. As soon as we found something promising we'd run a few checks online, if everything looked good we gave the owner a call and ask a few questions. We did this a couple dozen times before finding a car that was all green lights and still available. That car turned out to be the one we bought.

Research the major services required by your vehicle of choice. Services can be very expensive and the cost should be considered when buying a used vehicle. Finding a car in our price range with complete service records was the most difficult part of our search. If a service was skipped, the next scheduled service will be more expensive. It may also void the vehicle's warranty and most importantly it may compromise the reliability and safety of your ride.

Look for good balance of mileage and the cost of the next major service. A lower mileage vehicle that requires a major service soon is not as good of a deal as a vehicle that was just serviced but has more miles.

Check the reliability and safety ratings of the vehicle you are considering. These reports will tell you what problems are common, how they can be fixed, and what it costs. We used MSN Auto, Consumer Reports, Edmunds and Kelly Blue Book to research the reliability and safety ratings of various makes and models before deciding which to buy.

FOR MORE INFO SEARCH LIFEREMOTELY.COM

Choosing an Overland Vehicle

Companies like Carfax can provide service documentation for a fee, but only if the mechanic is registered with the company. In our experience, it's not likely you will get complete and accurate maintenance record using Carfax or similar service. The best way to determine a service history is to ask the owner or dealer for receipts. Private party sellers tend to have better records than a dealership. When in doubt, check the glove compartment.

A vehicle's title can tell you a lot about a car, inspect it carefully. If a vehicle has been written off due to collision, fire or flood damage or has been sold for scrap the title will be marked as branded, salvage or reconstructed. Such a vehicle might look new on the outside, but can contain hidden problems such as a bent frame or inferior replacement parts.

Sellers in the US are required by law to truthfully disclose the status of a vehicle's title. Take our advice and only buy a vehicle with a clean title, unless you are very comfortable working with cars and are willing to deal with a few surprises down the road, in which case, good luck!

Buying Your Vehicle

Paying a mechanic or employing the help of a friend to inspect the vehicle before you buy is highly recommended. Don't take the seller's word for it. If you don't know enough about cars to do an inspection yourself, you need someone to act on your behalf to help you make a smart decision. We used a company based in Portland, OR called eLemonators to do an on-the-spot inspection of our car.

Below is our advice for checking out a used car:

Make a list of questions to ask the seller and decide how much you are willing to spend. This will remind you of important details and stop you from over spending.

Bring a friend when you inspect and test-drive the vehicle. This adds a fresh pair of eyes and gives you a wingman to help with stressful sales pitches.

Don't believe everything the seller says, even if they look and sound honest. Ask for verification of every statement. There is rarely an "undo button" when you buy a used car. Only buy the vehicle if you are 100% satisfied.

Examine the vehicle inside and out. Drive it. Check the exterior for touch up paint. Check the seat belts, frayed or melted fibers may be evidence of an accident. Check the interior for obvious problems, such as a sagging headliner, cracked dashboard, and missing knobs, handles or buttons.

Open the hood and look to see that there is no obvious fluid leaking. Do a cold start and listen to the engine. If the engine has a knock you may not hear it if the engine is already warm.

When the engine is warm, check the tail pipe. Have your partner rev the motor and see if there is black, blue or white smoke coming out of the tail pipe. Black smoke is a sign of an air/fuel mixture problem. Blue smoke indicates oil burning. White smoke is evidence of water in the combustion chamber. All of these are all expensive repairs.

Beware of excuses. Don't fall for the "it's just a fuse" or "a broken light bulb" line. These are usually signs of electrical problems. If it was simple, the seller would have repaired it.

6

Vehicle Modifications

> Having the means to cook and sleep in or around your vehicle will undoubtedly pay for itself over the course of a long trip.

Modifications done to overlanding vehicles vary even more widely than the types of vehicles seen on the road. From adding extra storage and a place to sleep to completely retrofitting a van with hot water, solar power, a fridge, and a propane gas system. The possibilities are mindboggling. Some people just jump in and go, others spend more time and money outfitting their vehicles than they do traveling.

It's not hard to justify many modifications; you are essentially building yourself a house on wheels. Comfort, convenience and security are of utmost importance. Having the means to cook and sleep in or around your vehicle will undoubtedly pay for itself over the course of a long trip.

We spent roughly $2,000 modifying our 4Runner by adding a dual battery system, power inverter, fridge, roof rack, and beefing up the security. We also made a few cheap modifications to the rear storage area in an effort to make 18 months of packing and unpacking a bit less painful. Read more about the modifications we did to our 4Runner on our website.

Storage

Increasing the storage capacity of your ride should be top priority. The most popular modifications are done to the roof, hitch, or trunk. The goal is to have extra space to stash gear so that you can increase comfort and accessibility, thereby make your trip more enjoyable.

Having a place for everything and everything in its place is the only way to make the constant cycle of setting up and breaking camp bearable. We've spent the night in 80 different campsites and hotels during our trip to

Panama. That means we've packed and unpacked our car once every three days for nearly nine months. It gets old fast.

Roof Racks

If you have an SUV, van, or truck, chances are it either came with a roof rack or has the necessary hardware to install one. Easy to install clip-on and gutter-mounted racks are available for vehicles without existing track mounts or rails.

Our roof basket with Hi-Lift jack secured inside.

For general gear storage there are several options to choose from: a rack, a basket, or a box. A rack is the basic structure; typically two or three bars that span across or along your vehicle's roof. Add-on components are purchased to enhance a rack in order to mount a basket, box, spare tire, or outdoor gear such as surfboards, kayaks, bicycles and skis.

A basket is a low-cost roof rack add-on that increases your storage options. The major benefits are additional tie-down points and the ability to easily store smaller items. The downsides: there's no easy way to keep it all under lock and key, and everything is constantly exposed to the elements. We have a roof rack basket that holds our Hi-Lift jack and bulky disposable items like charcoal, firewood, water containers, and trash.

Roof rack boxes, commonly sold by Thule and Yakima in the US, are more expensive additions that give you the added benefit of having an enclosed, lockable container. They're an easy way to store extra clothing, gear and supplies without worrying about security and exposure to the weather.

Thule roof rack box on the Chevy Astro van of AnywherethatsWild.org

The downside to all roof rack setups is additional wind resistance, equating to lowered fuel efficiency and more noise while you're cruising down the highway. Generally speaking, the lower-profile the rack the less wind resistance it will cause. It is possible to install a fairing on the front of your rack to help combat the problem of reduced fuel efficiency and noise.

Packing and unpacking a roof rack can be a hassle. It's a lot easier to grab and repack gear in the back of your car. Strapping, tying and locking everything down takes considerably more time. We only use our roof rack to store items that will be quickly consumed or are rarely used.

Also keep in mind that all roof racks have a weight limit, as does your vehicle's roof. Storing heavy objects like spare tires, fuel, water and tools can be dangerous as they raise your vehicle's center of gravity, making it more likely to tip over. We've seen more than a few rolled Land Rovers in our time on the road.

Tailgate and Hitch Mods

Tailgate swingarm and hitch storage options vary depending on the type of vehicle. There are two basic setups; a gate attached to the side of the trunk that swings out like a door, or a rack that fits into the hitch mount and sits behind the rear bumper. These are the best options for storing spare fuel and water tanks outside your vehicle. The downside is that they may limit access to the back of the vehicle, requiring disassembly or removal before the trunk can be opened.

A swingarm is useful for storing a spare tire, Hi-Lift jack, and fuel and water tanks. It is by far the best place to store jerrycans safely outside your vehicle.

The major disadvantage is that it has to be opened before you can gain access to the back of your vehicle. It's also not a standard feature on most vehicles, and installing one may require additional work to strengthen the vehicle's frame and provide mounting points for the swingarm hinges.

Bumper with swing-out arm on www.LostWorldExpedition.com.com's Land Cruiser.

Hitch baskets are a good place to store tanks and bulky gear like sand tracks and tools. It is possible to purchase or build a hitch box that offers easy-to-access, secure and weatherproof storage of heavy items. Hitch mounts can also be purchased to carry bicycles, motorcycles, ATVs, or to extend large roof rack loads like tents and kayaks. The main drawbacks are, depending on the vehicle and gear stored, reduced ground clearance and difficulty accessing the trunk.

Trunk Storage Mods

The cheapest and most effective storage modification you can make to your vehicle is to optimize the space behind the passenger seats. Building shelves, drawers, and specialized storage compartments keeps everything organized. Crucially important considering how much time you will spend trying to find, use, and repack your belongings over the course of a long trip.

With a pickup or SUV the simplest modification is to build a shelf in the back to give you two levels of storage space. This allows you to store gear underneath that is not easily stacked or packed. Organized boxes, bins and bags go on top for easy access. Adding a fold-up shelf system or drawers makes it easier to reach and repack gear stored underneath.

It also helps to have an effective system of storage bins to maximize space and keep gear organized. As tent campers we prefer plastic bins, specifically Really Useful Boxes. They are easily removed, cleaned, and can be reorganized according to changing conditions. For more about how we store our gear see the articles in the Trip Gear section of our website.

Hinged gear storage area built in the back of our 4Runner.

Sleeping Area

We sleep in tents, so this isn't our area of expertise. Relatively speaking, our 4Runner's cargo space is small, especially given that there are three of us. We need eight square feet to store our tents, sleeping bags, mats, and sheets; roughly half the size of a small two-person mattress.

That said, the vast majority of overlanders sleep inside their vehicles. Whether it's a cushy RV mattress, a rooftop tent, a foam pad in bed of a truck, or a custom-built platform in the back of a van, overlanders prefer the comfort and security of a night's sleep inside their ride. The clear financial benefit is being able to snooze anywhere you park the car, making it much easier to avoid paying a hotel or campsite for a night's sleep.

Most sleeping setups break down into two categories: it's part of the vehicle already, or it isn't. If it isn't, your choice is to buy and install a rooftop tent, or build a plywood-supported, mattress-topped frame in the back of your vehicle.

Rooftop tents are very popular outside of the US, especially in Australia, Africa and New Zealand. They offer the best of both worlds, taking up zero space in the trunk while offering a more secure place to sleep off the ground. Configurations and prices vary widely, but most units attach easily to a stock roof rack and can be setup in minutes. The biggest downside is the cost. Small high-quality roof top tents start at around $1,000. Larger multi-person tents that include awnings, bug nets, and space for three or more people run upwards of $5,000.

Rooftop tent on the top of CapitolSouthbound.com's 4Runner.

Sleeping frames range from simple elevated platforms to pulley-winched contraptions that can be moved up and down to allow space for cooking and access to storage space underneath. It depends on your rig, and on how much patience you can maintain while constantly rearranging your stuff to make space to sleep. One thing is for certain: unless your vehicle is gigantic, you'll be sacrificing plenty of space to be able to bunk in the back. For two people in a mid-sized SUV, truck or van this isn't a big deal, but if you add a third person or downsize your ride there is little hope of having enough room.

Regardless of your choice of sleeping arrangements, keep in mind three very important nuisances: heat, bugs and rain. If you sleep inside your car, a 12v fan may very well be the best financial investment you make. Bug-proof netting is also worth its weight in gold. Familiarize yourself with the size and variety of biting insects in Mexico and Central America, especially no-see-ums.

Our waterproof, bug-proof, compact, and superbly ventilated Sierra Designs tent.

Do everything possible to build a bug-proof area to keep from being eaten alive while you sleep. Also, do your best to rainproof your sleeping area. You haven't experienced rain until you've successfully slept through a Costa Rican thunderstorm. Alternatively, you could just sleep in a waterproof, bug-proof, compact, and superbly ventilated tent for a fraction of the cost.

Power

Adding a bit more juice to your ride is a great way to make your travels more self-sufficient. Common options include installing additional batteries, solar panels, or a generator. Each has its trade-offs, but all serve the purpose of powering electronics such as a refrigerator, winch, extra lights, and portable appliances. It is also very handy for charging a laptop, phone, GPS and other overlanding toys.

Provided you aren't a certified electrician, sorting out the details and performing the modifications can be a harrowing experience. Fortunately, there are loads of resources available online, and chances are that step-by-step instructions can be found for your exact vehicle. We had the most luck finding help on 4x4, overlanding, and Toyota forums.

The biggest reason to consider expanding the electrical system in your vehicle is to avoid the possibility of draining the starter battery. Having an auxiliary battery or an electrical system separated from your starter battery means that you not only avoid being stranded, but you have the ability to jumpstart yourself if you run out of juice.

Plugs and Power Voltages

Not all power systems are created equal. North, Central and parts of South America use 110-120V with vertical blade plugs, often with a third round pin for ground. In Europe, the rest of South America and most other places in the world the voltages are 220-240V.

Why should you care? It's simple. If you have an electrical device, such as a battery charger that only runs on 110-120V or 220-240V, you might cross the Peruvian border and find it's useless. It is possible to buy voltage converters, although it's risky to use them as a permanent solution, especially for high-wattage devices. Avoid cheap 110/220V converters like the plague, they will eventually explode and possibly take your valuable electronics along with it.

Most electronics with built-in power supplies like laptops, phones and most anything that charges via a USB power adapter will work fine on any voltage between 110V and 240V. Check the fine print on the power adapter or on the back of the device. If not, it may be possible to buy second power adapter specifically for the device from the manufacturer that works on the other voltage.

Provided your electronics originate from North America, the drive through Central America will not be a problem. Voltages are 110-120V everywhere, and the plugs are all the same. With one exception: from Mexico south we frequently found plugs that did not include the ground pin, just the two blade plugs. Some of our gear, including our extension cord, power strip and laptops require the ground plug.

As an easy fix we picked up a couple cheap adapters called cheater plugs or ground plug adapters at a Mexican hardware store without a problem. It's generally regarded as unsafe to remove the ground as it protects you from electrical shock. However, all devices will continue to function normally, just don't go sticking your fingers in any power sockets.

A typical ground interrupt adapter (aka cheater plug).

The Simplest Options

If you aren't down with modifying your vehicle's electrical system, your best bet is to invest in a long heavy-duty extension cord. From there you can connect to a 12V battery charger and charge your battery. Or you can simply plug it into a power strip and use that to charge your electronics; power lights, and run small appliances. Approximately three quarters of the places we went had power nearby, the ones without were typically campgrounds in national parks with very limited facilities.

Dual Battery Systems

Simply put, the idea is to add a second battery to your car that is charged in conjunction with the starter battery. Overlanders choose dual battery systems to power 12V appliances such as a fridge, fans, lights, and winches. Connecting a power inverter to the system allows the use of 110-120V or 220-240V electronics.

Dual battery systems work by connecting both batteries to a solenoid that acts as a switch, electrically joining the two batteries and allowing both to be charged simultaneously while the engine is running.

Solenoids are either "dumb", meaning you must manually connect and disconnect the batteries. Or they are "smart" and will connect and disconnect automatically. Smart solenoids may also include built-in safety features such as only connecting the batteries after the engine has been running for a few minutes, ensuring your starter battery is always charged enough to turn the engine over. The obvious downside of a dumb solenoid is the result of forgetting to disconnect the two batteries after turning off your car. Both batteries will drain, potentially leaving you stranded.

Dual Optima batteries under the hood of our 1997 4Runner.

Not all batteries are created equal. The best choice for a dual battery setup is an auxiliary deep cycle or marine grade battery. Deep cycle batteries are designed to supply a constant amount of current over a long period of time, and to be deeply discharged repeatedly, something that will quickly ruin a normal car battery.

When buying a deep cycle battery, the statistic to look for is called RC, or reserve capacity. This is the number of minutes a battery can deliver up to 25 amps while keeping its voltage above 10.5 volts. The higher this number, the longer the battery will last. RC doesn't have much practical use aside from comparing brands.

There are too many factors involved to be able to figure out exactly how many hours your battery will put out enough juice. Ambient temperature, the minimum voltage required by your appliance, and the efficiency of your power inverter all play a part in determining how long a battery will last.

Wiring diagram for our dual battery system.

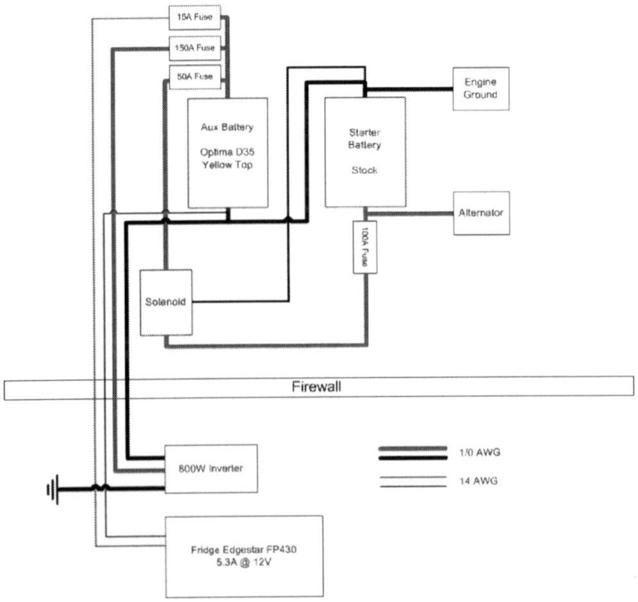

Above is the wiring diagram we created before installing a dual battery system in our 4Runner. The most difficult part of this experience was not doing the installation; it was finding the space under the hood of our car for a second battery, fuses and the solenoid. We purchased an Intelligent Solenoid from National Luna, a pricier option than most. However, it is well reviewed and since we were new to this, we appreciated the included guide. For more details on our dual battery setup, check out Part 1 and Part 2 of our installation process on our website.

Our Experiences

Our secondary battery powers an EdgeStar 43qt fridge and connects to an 800W power inverter that we use for charging our laptops, phone and camera batteries. The system we installed works wonderfully, but we've learned a few lessons after eight months on the road.

- Optima batteries are expensive, but they are workhorses. We can't easily do a real-life comparison with another brand; we just know our batteries work consistently, day after day, in less than ideal conditions.

- The hotter it is outside the quicker your battery will drain. It's a double-whammy if you're also powering a fridge inside your vehicle. Insulating your fridge and parking in the shade helps.

- On a really hot day (95F+), parked in the shade with the windows cracked, we get a little bit more than 24 hours out of our second battery while running only our fridge. Putting a bag of ice in the fridge will usually buy us another day, provided we don't use it all for cocktails.

- On cooler days (70F) our fridge will run two and half days. With a bag of ice in the fridge it will run for almost four days.

- Charging a 15" laptop on our power inverter will kill the battery in two hours. For this reason we typically only use our power inverter while driving.
- Idling our car will charge the battery in an hour and a half, although this is considered bad for the alternator. Driving at low RPMs will charge both batteries in under an hour.
- A battery monitor is a great addition to the setup. It gives us a heads up when our battery is going flat, and after six months of watching it we know exactly how the system will perform. We can anticipate how long it will take to charge, discharge, and how it handles different temperatures. A voltmeter works in a pinch, but it's a pain to pop the hood and check battery voltage frequently enough to get an idea of how the system performs under various conditions.

Solar Power

We've seen a handful of solar charging setups on our journey to Panama, and we are a bit jealous. We originally ruled this out as being overly expensive, but after asking a few questions it became obvious that for what we paid for our dual battery setup (around $1000) we could have had a solar setup for not much more money.

Solar panels on the roof of Nacho, read more about this setup at DriveNachoDrive.com

Solar panels are typically roof-mounted, although more convenient (but less efficient) fabric-like panels are also catching on. The idea of a solar setup is to use a solar panel to charge a battery that is located inside your vehicle. It doesn't have to be a standard 12V car battery; it can be something larger, or an array of 6V or 12V batteries, which gives you longer-lasting power in case of uncooperative weather.

Along with a battery and solar panels, a charge controller (also called a regulator), is necessary. Its primary job is to ensure that the solar panels do not overcharge the battery, and to prevent the battery from being deeply discharged. Both of these events will shorten the life of a battery.

The obvious concern with solar power is the lack of sunlight. However, with a big enough battery it's possible to last three or more days without sun. From our experiences driving to Panama, this would rarely be a problem.

For an excellent write-up on installing a solar system check out the detailed post from our friends at DriveNachoDrive.com.

Electrics

Provided you have the juice, adding a few gadgets to your ride will greatly improve your ability to camp, cook, entertain yourself, and keep your battery-powered electronics charged.

Refrigerators

Perhaps the most common, and in our opinion, the most useful piece of electronics you can add to your vehicle is a 12V fridge. Not a dinky plastic "cooler" that plugs into the cigarette lighter. We're talking about proper compressor-driven machines that can run at any temperature and stand up to the rigors of life in less-than-ideal conditions.

FOR MORE INFO SEARCH LIFEREMOTELY.COM

Installing a Fridge and Power Inverter in Our 4Runner

A decent fridge isn't cheap. But you can't put a price on the convenience and luxury of having a place to keep food and drinks cold. We've made more friends than we can count by pulling a bag of ice out of the back of our car during a sweltering day. "Oh, you have ICE?!?" "Why yes, yes we do."

ARB, Engel and Waeco are the big brand names. Without a doubt, models with Danfoss compressors are the highest recommended. We have a cheaper ($450 instead of $900) fridge made by Edgestar that not only fits perfectly in our vehicle, but also is the best fridge we've encountered on our way south.

Many problems have been reported with knockoffs as manufacturers such as Edgestar switched production to Chinese factories. While Edgestar fridges are generally well received, problems have been reported. There is a monstrous thread on Expedition Portal if you want more information.

Fridges run from tiny 15-quart models up to monster 80-quart fridge/freezer combo units used on sailboats. Prices range from $400 to $2000, with high-end average-sized fridges costing around $850. Our 43-quart Edgestar can hold four days worth of food and a dozen beers without a problem. We frequently drop a bag of ice in it, partially for drinks, and also to give our battery a break if we don't plan to drive for a couple days.

The downside to installing a fridge is that you must have a second battery. Running a fridge off of a starter battery in hot weather is asking for trouble.

Power Inverters

A power inverter allows you to transform 12V power supplied by a car battery to 110-120V that is used to power standard home electronics. We mounted a Cobra 800W inverter in the back of our 4Runner and use it to charge laptops, a cell phone, camera batteries and a kindle. It comes in handy when we're on a long drive or if we're stuck someplace without power.

However, it does quickly drain our battery. We can charge a laptop for about two hours before the battery calls it quits. Inverters are inherently inefficient, and have an overhead, draining the battery even if nothing is plugged in. Whenever possible, run electronics on 12V power, it's much more efficient than using an inverter.

It's best to install a power inverter as close to the battery as possible. The farther away the two are, the thicker the connecting cables need to be. Having no other choice, we were forced to use 0AWG cable to connect our power inverter to our battery, 13 feet away. Copper cables are expensive. And as we learned, the thicker they are, the more difficult they are to run through your vehicle.

Inverters are sold based on wattage. To calculate the wattage you'll need, add up the total current draw (amps) of all of the electronics you could feasibly have plugged in at the same time and multiply by 110 (assuming your inverter is 110V). The device or its power supply should list the amount of amps it draws, along with the voltages it supports. On a typical power supply you'll see something like "Input: 100-240W - 1.5A", the number 1.5 is what you want. As a good rule of thumb, add 25-50% to the total as some equipment momentarily draws more current as it starts up.

Watts = Amps x Volts

One last note about purchasing a power inverter, there are two types: pure sine wave and modified sine wave. Pure sine produces "cleaner" power, the same that you'd get from a wall socket. Modified sine wave inverters require your device's power supply to do more work to convert the incoming current into something manageable. It might generate more heat and buzz a bit, but generally speaking that's perfectly normal.

Some devices do have a problem with modified sine waves, but these are typically very old (5+ years) laptops, and scientific equipment like electron telescopes and medical imaging devices. Not the kind of stuff you'll need to bring on this trip. Moral of the story: at a third of the price, there's nothing wrong with a modified sine wave inverter for powering basic consumer electronics.

Suspension & Tires

No matter how careful you are, your vehicle's suspension is going to take a beating through Mexico and Central America. Your vehicle will also be hauling more than the usual amount of weight over long distances. Having a decent set of shocks and coils or leaf springs is essential. If they aren't in top shape the day you leave, you will be replacing parts on the road. A bad suspension system can also lead to other problems such worn-out bushings and wear and tear on steering components.

Match your suspension to your vehicle depending on how much weight you plan on carrying and how much off-roading you plan on doing. Don't go crazy unless you are a serious off-road enthusiast, in which case you probably shouldn't listen to our advice on this topic. For the rest of us, a good suspension system is about increasing safety by improving road handling and making your ride more safe and comfortable.

Decent all-terrain tires are also crucial. If your tires aren't in good shape before you leave, there's no better way to spend money to ensure you have a safe and successful trip. Don't forget to have a full-sized spare, and a way to repair and inflate after a flat. Certain tire sizes can be difficult to find in Central and South America.

Vehicle Recovery

An electric winch is the most convenient, safest, and most reliable way to get your vehicle unstuck. However, unless you plan on going off-road on very muddy, sandy, or snowy conditions it's not necessary for driving in Mexico and Central America. Electric winches come in all shapes, sizes and prices. The most common recommendation is to buy high quality to assure it will last, high-end models start at around $700.

To install a winch you will have to select a mounting system and winch cable capable of handling the pulling capacity of the winch. This often means beefing up the front bumper of your vehicle, further increasing the cost.

A Hi-Lift jack or a hand winch are much cheaper alternatives, but involve a fair amount of manual labor and additional safety hazards. A hand winch will do a better job of pulling you out of a bind, or through a rough patch of trail. It can pull a longer distance, while a Hi-Lift is limited to the size of the jack, about four feet.

A Hi-Lift is a more versatile tool, but is not considered a replacement for a winch due to its limitations. It is useful any time you need to lift, push, pull, or clamp something heavy. You can use it to change a tire, lift your vehicle over an obstacle, or pull yourself a short distance out of a hole.

Hi-Lift also makes accessories for specific situations. Jack protectors keep the mud and dirt out of the mechanical parts and mounting brackets are used to attach the jack to your vehicle. Additionally, the Lift-Mate accessory allows you to lift the vehicle from any wheel. This means you can lift all sides of your car without requiring jack points on the chassis.

Hi-Lift®

If you plan on seeking off-road challenges in out-of-the-way places, it's a good idea to bring both an electric winch and a Hi-Lift jack. After our positive experiences with a Hi-Lift in Africa, we opted to bring one on this trip and did not install a winch. The jack hasn't seen any use yet, but we're glad it's there in case of emergency. We've been on more than one rough backcountry road with very little non-equestrian traffic.

Security Upgrades

Considering all of your belongings will be riding with you in your car, it's a good idea to beef up security for added protection. With foreign plates your car is going to stand out on the street.

Lock Box

Lock boxes range from small metal letter boxes to full-on safes. It's a good idea to mount a small lock box out of sight to your vehicle to store passports, important documents, and spare cash. It can be an inconvenience at times, but it's a lot safer than the glove box.

We built a larger lock box to store our three laptops. It is bolted behind our fridge, next to the rear passenger seat. It's made of hardwood, several hundred 3" wood screws and covered in nondescript speaker fabric. The idea was to have a place where our laptops would be out of sight and stored safely in a padded box while we drive. It's strong enough to deter smash-and-grab jobs, and considering the cost of a metal safe of equivalent size, the price was right. Read more about how we built and installed our lockbox on our website.

Car Alarm

A good vehicle alarm will include keyless entry and a two-way remote. It's not a big deterrent considering the frequency car alarms are heard and ignored these days, but it might get you out of bed in time to save your stuff. We replaced our stock alarm with a Viper system that cost $400. It includes a two-way remote, backup battery and anti-carjacking features.

A kill switch can be added most vehicle security systems. Our switch works by activating the alarm while driving. When someone opens and closes a door before the alarm is deactivated, the siren starts. The next time the car is turned off the alarm system prevents the car from being started until a hidden button is pushed a preset number of times. The idea is to prevent carjackers from getting too far with your car.

In Africa we had a kill switch that was much more efficient, albeit a bigger pain. Every time you got in the car you had to push a hidden button. Failure to do that would interrupt the fuel line, stalling the car in the middle of the road. This isn't legal in the US and Canada, but we've heard of others having similar systems installed in Guatemala.

Security Cage

Many people who sleep inside their vehicle choose to build a metal cage to surround their sleeping area. This allows you to leave windows open and still have a safe night's sleep.

Attaching metal grating over your side and rear windows will give you a more secure place to keep your gear. Unless you have a closed cab, installing a fence behind the front seats will also be necessary. This is particularly

Security cage in the Chevy Astro van of AnywhereThatsWild.org.

handy if you are planning to ship roll-on roll-off on a cargo ship. This is a much cheaper way to send your car across continents, but it means you have to turn over your keys. Shipping roll-on roll-off is notoriously dangerous, many people are forced to empty their car or have it emptied for them while it's on the ship.

Locks

Lock nuts for your wheels are a cheap way to ensure nobody's going to walk off with your rims. One-way license plate screws do the same for your plates; kids have been known to walk off with foreign plates as souvenirs. Losing your plates in a foreign country is a hundred times the hassle of installing a couple screws.

A locking gas cap is another cheap and easy deterrent; it's also a good idea to carry the original gas cap as a spare. Gas stations are full service down here, and as we found out in Africa, you never know when the guy's going to forget to put the cap back on.

Cable locks are a good buy for securing gear to your roof rack or tailgate. We bought one to lock down our Hi-Lift jack. And if we ever put anything more valuable than a bag of charcoal up top, we'll be able to use it to secure that as well.

Tinted Windows

In some countries, Guatemala and Honduras for example, nearly every car window and windshield is tinted as dark as possible. If you are looking to pick up a cheap tint job, Guatemala is definitely the place to do it. But be careful with the rules in other countries, we've heard of people being given a hard time for having dark passenger windows farther south. We didn't tint our front windows, but we came close, mostly because of the heat rather than added security.

Awnings

A spot to relax that's out of the sun or rain and free of bugs is a priceless commodity in the tropics. An awning combined with mosquito netting is a great addition if you spend most of your nights in or around your vehicle.

Awnings range from custom-built rigs that offer little more than shade protection to professionally built and installed rigs that include bug nets and setup in seconds. We don't have an awning, although we've seen some truly inspired designs during our time spent driving to Panama.

Our camp setup and mesh awning in Mozambique, July 2008.

7

Tools, Spares and Safety Equipment

There are a lot of options when it comes to packing tools and spares. Some people can rebuild their engine with what they have in the trunk. Others choose to roll the dice and hope that if they breakdown a mechanic is nearby. To help with your decision we've included a list below, most of which we currently have stored in the back of our 4Runner.

This list is by no means comprehensive, our goal was to focus on a basic tool set, stock up on safety equipment, and bring only the smallest and most essential spares. We bought a 4Runner because it could be repaired everywhere, meaning we didn't have to haul a bunch of replacement parts across two continents.

Basic Tool Set

Ours tool kit consists of:

1. Big and small set of screwdrivers
2. Vice grips
3. Pliers
4. Adjustable wrench
5. Wire cutters
6. Epoxy
7. Super glue
8. Electrical & Duct tape
9. Voltmeter
10. Leather gloves
11. Socket set
12. Hex key set
13. Wrench set

FOR MORE INFO SEARCH LIFEREMOTELY.COM

Spares and Safety Equipment

What We Packed

Being Japanese, most of our vehicle is metric, however the modifications we've done include standard US sizes as well. To avoid bringing two full sets of wrenches and sockets we handpicked the sizes that fit to save space. We also sewed roll-up nylon cases for our tools to avoid bulky toolboxes, and to keep things from clanking around on bumpy roads.

Replacement Parts

People go off the rails when it comes to packing replacement parts. We can understand if you're driving a 1983 Mercedes sedan, but for us, only the bare essentials were deemed worthwhile. If you're driving a car that will be hard to find parts for, consider bringing a spare air, oil and gas filter, along with other small parts that are known problems for your vehicle such as wheel bearings, seals, water pump, fuel pump, starter, etc. Better yet, rethink your choice of vehicle, or accept the fact you may spend a lot of time broken down and in need of parts.

We've brought a selection of nuts and bolts, threaded to match common components in our vehicle. We also have a replacement set of belts, fuses, a couple lug nuts, and a gas cap. Our reasoning is that a spare part is worth bringing if it only cost a few bucks, could potentially save us from being stranded, and takes up very little space.

Fire Extinguisher, Road Triangles and Flares

An extinguisher should go without saying. In case it doesn't, you can pick one up for cheap in El Salvador before you cross into Honduras. You will get stopped, and you will get a ticket if you do not have a fire extinguisher while driving through Honduras. And if you are headed into South America, several other countries require them by law.

Another Honduran police scam is to ticket you for not having one (or sometimes two) warning triangles. They're cheap, small, and actually do come in handy if you breakdown in a bad spot. We've used them once or twice just to be safe. We didn't bring road flares, mostly because we never drive at night. We've found that in Latin American the universal daytime road flare is a tree branch cut and tossed into the road.

Jerrycans

Spare fuel tanks were a hotly debated topic for us. If you have the space outside your vehicle to strap on an empty can, go for it. If you don't, upgrading your tailgate storage or fitting an auxiliary tank under the car is a big expense. Storing fuel tanks on your roof is tricky business due to the added wind resistance and the danger of having a higher center of gravity.

We can go 330 miles on a tank of gas and can say with complete certainty that we have never needed more than that to hit the next station. With the exception of one stretch on the Baja peninsula, you'd have to try hard to go 150 miles without seeing a gas station. If we ever reach a stretch of road we know to be devoid of a fill-up, our plan is to purchase a temporary can, strap it to the roof, and then get rid of it.

Spare Tire and Tire Repair Kit

A full-sized spare, decent tire iron, puncture repair kit and air compressor are your tickets out of a bad situation. We're a fan of collapsible tire irons, not only are they infinitely more torque-worthy than the useless "L"-shaped wrench that comes with your car, they fit in nearly the same amount of space.

Having a full-sized spare tire is essential. You can't trust a donut on rough roads. Also, stopping to repair or fix-a-flat your tire may prove very inconvenient depending on your location or the time of day. Slapping on the spare will get you to the next stop with minimal fuss, giving you time to repair and test the puncture before heading off. Safety Seal truck tire repair kit is the most reliable and positively reviewed kit we could find.

A 12V air compressor will allow you to inflate a repaired tire. It's also useful to have on board if you need to drop tire pressure to handle soft roads. Most small compressors come with adapters to plug into the 12V cigarette adapter in your car, or can be wired with more convenient plugs to fit your auxiliary battery system.

Tow and Recovery Straps

A tow strap works like a seat belt. It does not stretch and is capable of carrying a constant weight over a variety of road surfaces. They aren't made for pulling stuck vehicles back onto the road. Using a tow strap for this purpose is dangerous because it can put an extreme amount of force on the strap and connecting hardware.

A recovery strap works like a rubber band. It stretches and stores a huge amount of energy. When it reaches a specific tension, it recoils. Recovery straps are made for unsticking stuck vehicles.

You should buy a recovery strap that has loops on both ends rather than hooks, and pick up a couple heavy-duty shackles for connecting it to your vehicle. The strap must be attached to a secure place on the vehicle's frame. If you don't have recovery points on the front and back, they can be purchased and bolted or welded to your vehicle's frame for little cost. Scrap yards are a great place to pick them up for cheap.

Recovery straps are safer and more useful than tow straps for most overlanding applications.

Sand Tracks and Bridging Ladders

Sand tracks are used to give you more traction when the road turns to mush. They're used in soft sand, deep mud, and snowy conditions. You drop them down in front of your wheels and drive over them to safer ground. Bridging ladders are much stronger than sand tracks and are used to create a ramp, or to cross deep and narrow washouts and crevasses.

Due to their size and weight, we chose not to bring tracks or ladders on this trip. The combination of our 4WD, recovery gear, and the fact we don't go looking for trouble means we don't have to be as careful as some. If we see a patch of soft sand or deep mud we stop and check it out. If it looks risky, we head the other way. There has never been a patch of road on this trip where tracks or ladders would have come in handy. We've met others on the road with tracks that have never been used.

8

Gear

FOR MORE INFO SEARCH LIFEREMOTELY.COM

Kitchen Gear

Toiletries and First Aid Gear

Tools and Spares

Camping Gear

Personal Bins and Daypacks

Fishing Gear

Extra Stuff

What you bring on this trip is entirely your decision. We've seen people happily making do with the bare minimum and others with vehicles filled to the brim. Available space, whether or not you plan to camp, and how much you can live without are the deciding factors when choosing what to pack. We can emphatically say from experience that the gear you bring isn't going determine how successful and happy your travels are.

The cliché tip is that less is more. If you've done any amount of traveling, especially backpacking, you understand the benefits of packing light. But it bears repeating: the more gear you have to load, unload, repack and bounce down the road with, the more frustrated you will become. There's no point in letting useless junk ruin the mood.

With the exception of high-quality camping gear, you can pick up just about anything in cities throughout Latin America. If in doubt, don't bring it. Especially if it's something you could buy at Walmart. Yeah, they have those down here too.

Test Everything

Our best advice is to spend a lot of time at home packing, unloading and repacking. Once you're satisfied, go on trial runs to work out the kinks. We did at least a dozen rounds of test packing, and went on several long weekend trips before heading south.

The test runs told us what we did right and wrong, helped us eliminate unnecessary equipment, and reminded us of what we forgot to bring. By the time we hit the Mexican border we were convinced we'd made the right decisions and it's been smooth sailing ever since.

Gear We Love

> **FOR MORE INFO SEARCH LIFEREMOTELY.COM**
>
> Central and South America Full Packing List

Choosing gear is completely subjective. We're not here to advocate a specific brand or tell you what you can't live without. Below is a list of equipment that has worked superbly well for us. Your mileage may vary.

Really Useful Boxes – $18 to $25 per box

These plastic bins currently hold 90% of our worldly belongings. They come in every size, shape and color imaginable. They're durable, stackable, don't waste a lot of space, and fit perfectly in our car.

Bug Repellent – $17 for three two-ounce bottles

We stock up on bottles of 100% DEET to save space. When the biters come out we dilute it with water to roughly 15%, shake, and apply. As campers without a bug-proof shelter aside from our tents, we can't live without it. We also use lemon eucalyptus spray to combat flies, especially no-see-ums that tend to ignore DEET.

Occasionally we'll also break out a mosquito coil in our cooking area if the bugs are especially thick. If you run out, it's possible to buy bug spray and coils in most supermarkets in Latin America.

Folding Grill Rack – $30

We like to grill, and this little guy was a perfect solution to our space problems. Although charcoal is very easy to come by, we haven't seen many other overlanders grilling on an open fire. We grill every chance we get.

Folding Shovel – $42

A shovel goes hand-in-hand with the grill rack. We use it to dig fire pits, clear off tent sites, and dig out other people's cars when they get stuck in the sand.

Spice Bottles – $42 for 12 bottles

We eat well, and a big reason for this is our collection of a dozen spice bottles. Chocked full of flavor crystals and easily packable. We searched long and hard, and paid a pretty penny to find a set of food-safe square bottles, but there are no regrets.

Unlocked 3G Modem and Router – $69 and $51

Need internet wherever you are? An unlocked 3G USB modem is the way to go. It's cheap, and once you figure it out, pretty easy to setup in every country. If you need to share a connection with more than one device, grab a router that will work with a 3G stick.

Unlocked Cell Phone – $190

A phone can come in very handy at times. It's a necessity for us because of our work commitments. We also use it to get in touch with our overlanding friends, to call parks or hotels for more information, and to call home on Mother's Day. A smart phone with a prepaid data plan can be very useful for checking maps and email along the way, but is far from a necessity.

Wireless Extenders – $28

A backup wireless card with a beefier antenna is a great investment. We've used it many times to access wifi signals from our campsites. It's handiest when we encounter wireless connections that don't play nice with our laptop's built-in wireless card. Having a backup wifi card means connectivity problems are rarely our fault.

A Good Sleeping Bag – $150 to $600

The tropics are all about sunshine and sweat, but once you drive into the mountains it gets downright cold. It's hard to put a price on a good night's sleep. For more info on how to choose a good sleeping bag see our article, "Sleeping Bags: The good, the bad, and the extra fluffy."

Silk Travel Sheet – $52

As tent campers, these sheets have come in handy many times. Inside a sleeping bag they will keep you warmer. And when it's 85 degrees out at night, it's nice to have a thin layer that won't instantly have you sweating. We've also used our sheets in seedy hotels/hostels with questionable cleanliness and potential bug problems.

Kindle – $139 to $189

Books are big and heavy, and although hostel book exchanges are easy to come by, one can only take so much of Dean Koontz and Tom Clancy. Perhaps the best part of a Kindle for a traveler is the free 3G. The browser isn't fancy, but it's enough to surf basic web pages and check email. It does not work in Belize or Costa Rica, but that may change in the near future.

Maps – $12 per map

We bought paper maps from Reise Know-How, a German map publisher and the most recommended and up-to-date road maps we could find. Locals are shocked at how accurate they are. We've even impressed a few tour guides.

We also have a Garmin 60GSX GPS. It's a bit dated, but it's cheaper and has better satellite reception than the newer version. If you have a Garmin GPS you can get free maps online from Open Street Maps and Cenrut that work fairly well.

EdgeStar Refrigerator – $410

One of the best investments we made for this trip. It holds three to four days of food plus a twelve pack or a bag of ice. EdgeStar has mixed reviews, especially when it comes to customer service, but we haven't had a single problem yet (knock on wood). At half the price, and a perfect fit for our car, it was an easy choice for us over more popular manufacturers.

Leatherman – $58

Infinitely useful and with a lifetime warranty, it sees action almost every day. Repairing glasses, fixing a laptop, making sandwiches in the back of the car, taking apart a watch, there's not much it can't do.

Water Container – $15

This 2.5-gallon water container is enough to get us through a couple days. We refill it with either treated or bottled water when needed. It's square, so it fits well in our car, and has a good spout design that makes it easy to refill water bottles and rinse dishes.

Gear Other Overlanders Love

We recently asked a German couple we encountered what their favorite thing was they brought on their trip. After four years on the road, they each replied separately that it was their significant other. While it's true that the people you bring with you on the trip are far more important than any given piece of gear, most overlanders have at least one item that they swear by.

James and Lauren of HomeontheHighway.com heap mountains of praise upon their Endless Breeze Fan-Tastic Fan, claiming that it is the best fan ever created and the one item they would not be able to live without. Many other overlanders agree that a good fan is the best investment you can make before starting on this trip, especially if you plan to sleep inside your vehicle.

Brianna and Logan of PanAmNotes.com give the nod to their Garmin Nuvi as their favorite piece of equipment. They also credit their three cubic foot fridge as being a huge (literally) asset. We agree that not having to choose between cold beer and a couple extra meals is a nice perk.

In their blog post "Overlanding Gear: The 11 Things we LOVE and use everyday," Caesar and Danni of CapitolSouthbound.com list their favorite pieces of gear. The top spot belongs to their Hydro Flask Stainless Steel Insulated Drinking Bottle. Nothing beats water that stays cold all day!

Brenton and Shannon of RuinedAdventures.com state that their 24-year-old 4Runner, aka "The Border-Runner" is their favorite piece of equipment. They give a second vote to their roof-mounted Endless Breeze fan.

9

Paperwork

Crossing international borders with your own vehicle requires a pile of paperwork, and the organizational skills to keep it all manageable. It's also crucial to keep your paperwork safe, especially originals. Losing a passport, vehicle title, or import permit will certainly ruin your day.

We keep our passports and copies of everything stored in a lockbox with our laptops. All other paperwork is sorted into small manila envelopes and kept in the glove box. One envelope holds our insurance paperwork, vehicle title, registration, and extra copies of this paperwork. Another holds documentation from previous countries, and a third holds important receipts, such as work done on the car.

Always be careful when handing over original paperwork! Never let it out of your sight.

Our current vehicle permit and other required paperwork, such as country-specific insurance, is loose in the glove box for easy access. Along with a driver's license, these are the first things the police want to see after being stopped at a checkpoint.

Paperwork You Will Need

- **Driver's license.** Having a spare expired license to give to sketchy cops is a good idea. An international driver's license is good for the same reason, but isn't required to drive in Mexico and Central America.

- **Passports.** If you are a resident of another country, bring that paperwork as well. Kobus' US resident (green) card has helped him avoid paying visa fees.

- **Immunization documentation.** Some South American countries require proof of yellow fever vaccination, especially if you have ever visited a country where yellow fever is endemic. Mexico and Central America do not require any vaccinations, but they are still a good idea to get.

- **Car title and registration.** We've needed the car title at every crossing, and the registration only when entering Honduras. Make sure the driver's name is on the car title. If it isn't, you will need at a minimum a notarized letter from the owner and may have additional hoops to jump through at border crossings.
- **Credit or debit card.** It should go without saying, but you'd be surprised. ATMs are doubtlessly the best way to get money abroad. You may need to present a card at some border crossings to prove "fiscal solvency", otherwise a bank statement showing a healthy balance should suffice.
- **Insurance paperwork.** The international insurance we bought in the US hasn't kept us from having to buy mandatory insurance at certain borders, but it's a good idea to have on hand in case someone asks.
- **Copies of everything!** At a minimum you will need a copy of the driver's license, passport and vehicle title at almost every border crossing. Honduras requires three copies of everything you have.
- **Electronic copies.** Make copies of everything and save them on your computer and online. Send a copy to someone back home who you can reach easily, just in case.

10

Insurance

Opinions are varied as to the benefits of insurance for a trip of this nature. We opted to buy international car insurance, health insurance, and a renter's policy to cover our belongings back home. Many long-term travelers prefer to use their bank account as insurance, and there's nothing wrong with that choice, we simply didn't want to take the risk.

The biggest argument against health insurance is that care is much cheaper and in many cases just as good in Mexico and Central America. We bought health insurance because we're from the US. Our biggest fear is being medevac'd home without insurance and in need of serious medical care.

FOR MORE INFO SEARCH LIFEREMOTELY.COM

The Truth about all Types of Travel Insurance

Car insurance is not advantageous for some overlanders. If your car isn't worth much, neither is an insurance policy that covers anything but liability. If it's old, chances are it won't be insurable for theft or fire. Also, in some cases, modifications, upgrades, and belongings inside your vehicle won't be covered by a car insurance policy.

On the other hand, property or renter's insurance is something everyone should have. It's cheap, and it covers everything at your registered address (back home) and anything where you currently reside (in your car or hotel room). If our car gets stolen or burns to the ground with all of our stuff in it, we're only out the deductible. At a cost of $25 per month, this was an easy decision to make.

Vehicle Insurance

If you are driving in the US and Canada, vehicle insurance is required. Policies in the US will typically cover your car in Canada, and visa versa. It's a good idea to check first, and let them know where you're headed; your premiums may need to be adjusted to allow for coverage.

Liability insurance is required in Mexico and by law must be purchased from a Mexican company. It's best to take care of this before you cross the border. It can be purchased at the border but you will pay more. Chances are they won't ask for it at the border, but police will certainly want to see it if they stop you down the road.

We bought Mexico insurance online from Sanborns for $280. Policies are sold by the day, month, six-months and annually. Because we planned to spend at least 60 days in Mexico, it was cheaper for us to buy a six-month policy rather than pay for two one-month increments.

Car insurance south of Mexico is a mixed bag. Some countries require liability coverage and force you to purchase it at the border, usually for less than $20.

Finding third-party vehicle insurance to cover us in Central and South America proved to be a bit more of a challenge. We ended up finding insurance sold by Insurance Consultants International that covers us in every country except Belize, Costa Rica, Nicaragua and Colombia. Each of those four countries require that you buy liability insurance at the border. It may also be possible to buy additional collision, theft and fire insurance from brokers within those countries.

US and Canadian car insurance will not cover you in Mexico or beyond.

Our policy cost $1,850 for a year of coverage with a deductible of $250, $500 for collision. It covers fire, theft, liability, collision, some medical, and property damage. It does not cover belongings inside our car, but it does cover the modifications we've done to prepare for this trip. The policy also states that any car older than 15 years will not be insured for fire or theft, we squeaked by on that one. One year was the maximum length of coverage we were able to purchase before we left, after that it can be extended by one-month increments indefinitely.

Health Insurance

If you're an American, purchasing health insurance that covers you in the event you have to return home for medical treatment is a smart move. Not all international health insurance policies cover the US, and those that do are more expensive. The good news is that if you're used to paying for insurance in the US, it's likely you'll spend less on a policy that assumes you're going to spend most of your time out of the country.

Health insurance is not travel insurance. Travel insurance packages may include health insurance, but they are limited in coverage and may not be renewable for the entire duration of your trip. Baggage and trip cancellation insurance may be included, but these are virtually useless to an overlander. Rather than buy a travel policy, buy individual health and property insurance and avoid paying for services you will never use.

Check Out These Insurance Companies:

International Medical Group

Seven Corners

STA Travel

Travel Guard

World Nomads

ihi Bupa

HTH Worldwide

Medical, emergency evacuation/repatriation, and accidental death and dismemberment insurance are the most useful components of a health insurance plan. Our policies with International Medical Group cover all three, up to a maximum of $5 million, with no copay, and a deductible of $2,000. For a one-year policy the guys paid $650 each. It cost Jessica $850 because maternity care is included.

Our theory is that healthcare is cheap in the countries we're visiting, so unless it's something very serious we have no problem paying out of pocket. However, if it's major, and especially if it requires a trip back home, we want coverage. A high-deductible policy with no copay and US coverage fit the bill.

Watch out for:

- Most policies come with a list of excluded countries. We've seen policies sold as "worldwide coverage" that exclude a few dozen countries.
- Certain states in the US, including our home state of Washington, have laws that prohibit the sale of certain types of health insurance policies. Travel insurance companies we've used in the past were unable to sell us policies that lasted more than a year for this reason.
- "Dangerous" activities aren't included. This could mean surfing, playing football, mountain biking, climbing over 20,000 feet, scuba diving or flying in a small aircraft. Essentially any activity where you are most likely to be injured. Some policies offer an extra rider that will cover some of these activities for an additional fee.
- As with most health insurance policies sold in the US, if it's pre-existing or involved drugs or alcohol, your chance of coverage is zero.
- Our policy states that if we seek medical attention, we must immediately notify our insurance provider. Failure to do so may result in a declined claim.
- Natural disasters, wars, and acts of terrorism may be not be covered by evacuation insurance.
- Some insurance may require that you "pre-authorize" emergency medical transportation with the company given a doctor's recommendation. This has the potential to be an insanely stressful situation.

Property Insurance

If you have an existing renter or homeowner policy, check to see if they will cover your belongings while you travel. If you are keeping a house back home, it shouldn't be a problem. Typically, property insurance covers everything in your registered address, along with anything "with" you. This means anything in your car, hotel room, or campsite.

If you are a renter, it's hard to get your belongings covered if you put them in a storage unit. It's best to move everything to a friend or family member's house. It may be cheaper to have him/her extend their property insurance policy to cover your belongings rather than opening or transferring a renter insurance policy. It's also a good idea to go out of your way to make this person's life better, they are doing you a huge favor. We spent a week and a chunk of change refinishing our mom's garage in exchange for a few hundred square feet of storage space.

Watch out for:

- Limits on electronics coverage. Some policies max out at $500, especially baggage policies. A fraction of the cost of one laptop.
- Exclusions, particularly on jewelry, glasses, and sporting equipment. This is most common with travel insurance policies, not property insurance.
- If you own a business, chances are that nothing your company owns will be covered by a homeowner or renter policy. You will need a separate policy.
- Coverage for loss. Unless it's stolen or burnt to the ground, and reported to the authorities, your chance of coverage is minimal. Some companies may allow you to pay extra for the "oops I lost it" waver. Worth the extra small fee for things like wedding rings.

11

Health

Staying healthy and being safe on the road is 20% preparation and 80% common sense. We're here to help you be prepared; you'll have to supply the rest. Know what the risks are, what diseases are common, and how to prevent them. Pack a first aid kit, learn about food safety, and have more than one way to purify water. Be ready to deal with the unexpected and posses enough information to let your common sense do the rest.

Vaccinations

This information is for reference only. See your doctor or travel medical clinic for a full consultation. Ask as many questions as possible, most travel doctors have a wealth of knowledge about how to deal with illnesses, insects, and what to avoid eating and drinking. Check out the CDC's travel website for the most up-to-date information about vaccinations and health risks.

FOR MORE INFO SEARCH LIFEREMOTELY.COM

Vaccines & Immunizations for International Travel

If you are in the US and have insurance, make sure you get everything necessary for living in the US before you mention that you will be traveling. Odds are your insurance will not pay for a yellow fever shot. But they are likely to pay for hepatitis A, B and tetanus shots if you ask for them as a soon-to-be college student, medical trainee, or simply a paranoid adult. Vaccinations for the purpose of traveling were not covered by our policies and cost us roughly $200 per person.

Yellow Fever

Required for entry into some South American countries, especially if you have recently been to a country where yellow fever is endemic. You will receive a small yellow international immunization card; keep it with your passport.

Yellow fever is contracted via mosquito bites, and is prevalent in the lowlands of South America and Panama. Vaccination lasts for 10 years.

Tetanus-Diphtheria-Pertussis

One shot lasts 10 years. Better than being stuck by a five-inch needle after stepping on a rusty nail.

Rabies

Recommended by the CDC for long-term travelers. Given the number of stray animals in Latin America, it may be a good idea.

Hepatitis A

Usually contracted through infected food or water. Highly recommended for travelers going to Central and South America.

Hepatitis B

Contracted through blood or other bodily fluids. Highly recommended. Requires a series of shots over several months. Can be taken in conjunction with the hepatitis A vaccination called Twinrix. This is now a required vaccination for kids in the US, but if you're over 25 it's not likely you have it.

Typhoid

Usually acquired by food or water that has been contaminated with feces, the typhoid vaccine is recommended for travel outside of the western world. You have the option to get a shot, or take a series of tablets over the course of a week. The shot lasts longer, up to 5 years, plus you can't drink alcohol while taking the tablets.

Malaria

Our Choice

Cases of malaria do occur in lowland Mexico and Central America, however the CDC considers these areas at low risk. We are not taking anti-malarial medications on this trip.

FOR MORE INFO SEARCH LIFEREMOTELY.COM

Malaria Risks and Prevention

We spent four months in Africa experiencing what those drugs are like in terms of hassle, expense, and side effects. We decided it wasn't worth it. We know the signs. If someone gets sick, we get a test kit, see a doctor, and get patched up. Central America isn't like Africa; you are rarely more than an hour or two from help.

About Malaria and Preventative Drugs

The deadliest animal in the world is the female malaria-carrying mosquito. Malaria is a parasite, there are no vaccines, but if treated quickly it can be cured. To make matters worse, the parasite has evolved into several strains, some of which are resistant to preventative drugs. Mexico and Central America are considered chloroquine-sensitive areas; do not take chloroquine medications to prevent malaria in these countries.

FOR MORE INFO SEARCH THE CDC WEBSITE

Malaria Map

Malaria Risk and Drug Resistance By Destination

Choosing a Drug to Prevent Malaria

Fever, chills, headache, muscle pain, nausea and vomiting are all common symptoms of malaria, the same as having the flu. It is impossible to diagnose malaria without a blood test. Thankfully, most pharmacies in countries where malaria is present sell cheap and effective test kits. If you're traveling in rural areas for extended periods of time, it's worth picking up one or two.

Pills must be taken daily or weekly and typically should be started two to seven days before taking effect. You also must continue taking the drugs between one week and four weeks after returning home. The medications also have a limited shelf life, especially if exposed to high temperatures and sunlight.

If you do decide to take malaria medications, consider buying them Mexico or Central America where they are much cheaper. Be warned that the available medications will change, and given their short shelf life, you may be forced to switch medications as you travel.

First Aid Kit

Your first aid kit should contain the supplies you need to manage existing medical conditions, prevent illnesses related to travel, and take care of minor health problems as they occur. While first aid supplies are easily purchased at pharmacies throughout Mexico and Central America, it's a good idea to have well-stocked kit with you at all times.

FOR MORE INFO SEARCH LIFEREMOTELY.COM

First Aid Kits: What You Need and Why

Our First Aid Gear

Prescription Drugs

If you take prescription drugs, bring the prescription with you, along with plenty of extra medication. To avoid problems with the authorities, make sure everything is packaged in the originally labeled bottle. Never carry a prescription belonging to someone else. In Latin American pharmacies it is possible to buy many prescription medications over-the-counter for a fraction of US prices.

Original Packaging

Cut off the back of the box of over-the-counter medications in case you need to explain to an official what it's for. Also, having the scientific name of the medication handy will make it easier to restock. Brand names may become unfamiliar once you leave home.

Full-Spectrum Antibiotic

Take the time before you leave to see a doctor and get a prescription for a broad-spectrum antibiotic such as Cipro. It kills the bugs that cause diarrhea. We've used it on more than one occasion. It doesn't matter how careful you are, if you spend enough time down south, it will happen.

First Aid Kit List

Medications

- Prescription drugs you are taking
- Average pain and headache medicine: acetaminophen, aspirin or ibuprofen
- Diarrhea drugs: immodium
- Normal upset stomach drugs: mild laxative, antacid
- Cold or congestion drugs: decongestant, cough suppressant/ expectorant, throat lozenges
- Antihistamine: Benadryl tables, itch cream
- Motion sickness tablets: Dramamine
- Broad spectrum antibiotic: Cipro
- Sleep aids: Tylenol PM

Basic First Aid Supplies

- Antiseptic wipes
- Disposable gloves, 2-3 pairs
- Variety of adhesive strips (band aids)

- Variety of sizes of sterile gauze pads
- Rolled gauze
- Tape
- Cotton swabs
- Antiseptic cream
- Iodine, hydrogen peroxide or alcohol disinfectant
- Tweezers
- Scissors
- Thermometer
- Saline eye drops
- Moleskin or other blister prevention pads
- Elastic bandage (ACE bandage)
- Hydrocortisone cream
- Malaria test kit
- Sewing kit
- Basic first aid book

It's a big list, but it packs small. Keep in mind that most of these items can be restocked as you travel and may be cheaper outside the US and Canada. You don't need to take enough for your entire trip, just enough to get you to the next town or medical facility.

Check out the CDC's travel health kit online for more information.

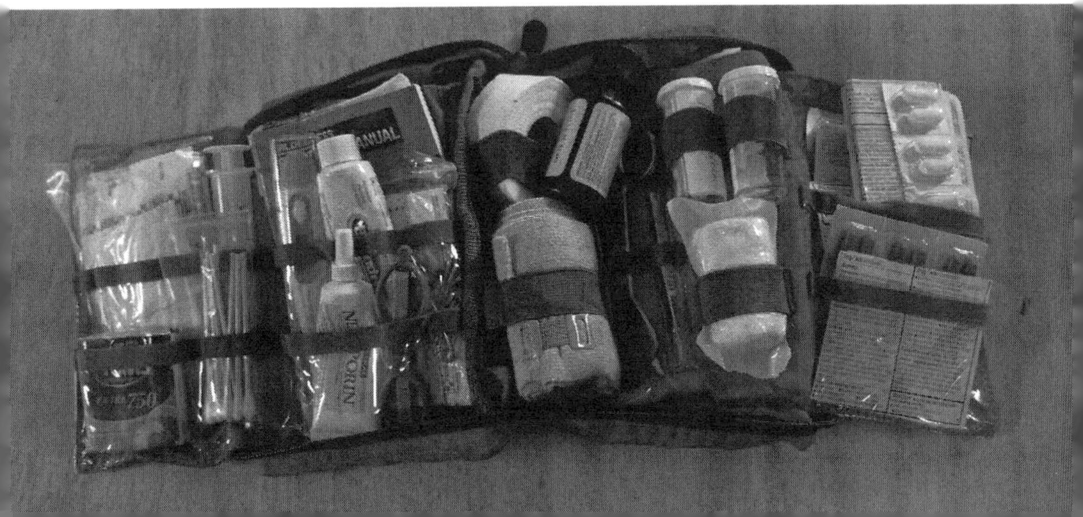

Food and Water

Food and water-borne illnesses are a common occurrence for travelers in Latin America. Staying healthy is a matter of knowing what is safe to eat and drink, and how to properly store, handle and cook your own food.

It is best to assume tap water is unsafe to drink until told otherwise. We found that the water is treated in densely populated areas of Costa Rica and Panama, and in big resorts. Anywhere else is not likely to have safe drinking water, you have to buy it or purify it.

Purifying Water

If you plan to spend a lot of time camping, have more than one way to purify water. Carrying a bottle of iodine tablets along with your primary means of purifying water is the best bet. Iodine tablets take up very little space and work for all types of water, no matter how cold or dirty. In a pinch you can also boil water; one minute should do it, up to three minutes at high elevations.

FOR MORE INFO SEARCH LIFEREMOTELY.COM

Preventing Traveler's Diarrhea

Treating Traveler's Diarrhea

Devices for cleaning water are broken down into three categories: purifiers, filters and ultraviolet. A filter will remove sediment, parasites, and bacteria, but unlike purifiers and UV devices it will not kill viruses such as hepatitis A and B. REI has a great write up that compares the purifies and filters, and offers plenty advice for choosing the right setup: part 1 and part 2.

We use a Steri-Pen for water purification. It runs on batteries and uses UV light to kill the bad bugs. It's doesn't require maintenance aside from battery changes. The downside is that it takes a while to purify a large volume of water, and it does not filter water to remove sediment.

For the most part we buy water. In every country north of Costa Rica it was the cheapest option for us. It costs more for batteries for our Steri-Pen than it does to pick up 10 liters of bottled water from a supermarket every couple days. For most cooking applications and for doing dishes we don't bother to filter water, just soap and air dry.

Food Safety

Food poisoning is a very real problem and will knock you out for at least a couple days. We've managed to avoid it thus far, but we are ever vigilant when cooking and eating out.

Here are a few tips to keep the bad bugs off your plate:

- It should go without saying, but wash your hands! Hand sanitizer or wet wipes are good in a pinch.
- Unpurified ice, meat and produce that's either unwashed or washed with dirty water are the most common sources of food poisoning and traveler's diarrhea.
- Eat where the locals eat. No restaurants become popular by poisoning their neighbors. But be aware that residents have a resistance to some bugs that could ruin your day.
- Talk to people about where to eat and what foods may be a problem for foreigners. Hotel staff and hostel owners are a great source of this information.
- Be careful when buying street food. That said, food from the wagon can be safer than you'd think. This is especially true if you see it being cooked. You don't often have this luxury in a sit-down restaurant. When in doubt, order what the guy in front of you ordered. If it looks like it's been sitting in a sun a few hours: pass, or ask for a fresh serving.

- Be extra careful of buying drinks on the street like punches, fruit juices, and shaved ice. Always ask if the water and ice is purified.
- Know what to look for when buying fresh veggies and fruit. Avoid fruit that has been cut open. Produce that must be peeled or boiled are your safest options.
- Always wash produce that will be eaten raw with purified water.
- Cook for yourself. Know how to properly clean produce and cook meat. Err on the side of over cooking meat unless you're sure of its origins and that it's been properly handled.
- Use a fridge or cooler to store meat, dairy products, and anything else that doesn't do well in hot weather.
- Use your nose. If it smells bad, don't eat it. We sniff-check everything before putting it in the pan. Much of the meat, especially poultry, does not seem to last as long as it did back home.
- If you want to cook seafood, buy it and eat it the same day. The freshest fish will not smell strongly of fish, and the gills will be bright red. For the tastiest and freshest seafood imaginable, hang out on the beach in a small fishing village.
- We have a rule: no eating raw fish if we are more than one hour from the ocean. It doesn't matter where we are. We wouldn't eat sushi in Kansas, nor would we eat ceviche in Guatemala City. We're not saying there's something wrong with all ceviche in Guatemala City, it's simply not a risk we are willing to take for the sake of raw fish.

Part 2:

ON THE ROAD

12

Handling Money

Cash is still king in much of Latin America. Plenty of places do accept plastic, but the vast majority of budget hotels, restaurants, campgrounds and small stores will only take cash. How you go about getting that cash, what you do with it, and how you keep it safe are important to consider. As is developing a method for handling money that supports your financial situation.

Banking and ATM Fees

ATM cards are by far the safest, easiest, and most convenient way to access cash. Traveling with a lot of cash is risky, and traveler's checks aren't likely to be around much longer. Finding ATMs throughout Mexico and Central America is quite easy. Occasionally we will come across a town with only a single ATM. Once or twice we've been far enough off the grid that there was no way to get money from the wall. Guidebooks tend to give ample warning when ATMs are scarce.

> Odds are your checking account from home is not a wise choice to take on the road.

Bank fees can be very high for international travelers. Odds are your checking account from home is not a wise choice to take on the road. Unless you want to lose 3% of your money every time you use your card, and $5 every time you withdraw money from a machine. Luckily, if you shop around, you should be able to avoid most of these costs.

Bank charges can be broken down into ATM fees and percentage-based "currency exchange" fees. There are two types of ATM fees, those charged by your bank, and fees levied by the owner of the ATM. You can find out owner fees when you withdraw money from the ATM. And you can contact your bank for information about international ATM withdraw and currency exchange fees.

The best bank accounts will not charge any fees for using an ATM and will also reimburse owner fees. We have checking accounts with Charles

Schwab that not only have zero fees for using an ATM internationally, but also reimburse most fees levied by the ATM owner. This saves us roughly $30 every month. The one exception is when we use an out-of-network machine that does not have a Plus (Visa network) logo.

FOR MORE INFO SEARCH LIFEREMOTELY.COM
Handling Credit Cards, Cash and Bank Accounts while Traveling Internationally

Visa and MasterCard charge a 1% fee for international withdraws. On top of that your bank may charge another 1-2%. With the right account your bank will not charge any percentage fees, and will not pass the 1% credit card company fee on to you. Regardless, a 3% fee is still better than most money changing services.

Carrying Plastic

Before you leave, tell your bank you are traveling. They will probably need to "activate" your card for international use. For security reasons, most banks will block your card if they see overseas charges coming through unexpectedly. This is easy to fix by calling your bank, but it can happen at very inconvenient times. If you're in a foreign country when this happens, check the back of your card for an international collect number.

It's a good idea to have both major brands of cards (MasterCard/Cirrus and Visa/Plus) with you, although we have had no problems using our Visa cards everywhere we've wanted to be.™

Avoid carrying more than one card on your person. If you need two cards, keep them in separate places. Write the number of your bank down somewhere other than the back of your card. If you lose a card you'll want to let your bank know immediately so that they can cancel it. You aren't liable for charges made to your card after you report it stolen.

> Before you leave, tell your bank you are traveling.

We've seen two cases of fraudulent charges made to cards on our trip. Both happened in Guatemala and were likely due to hijacked ATM machines. It's a good idea to regularly check your bank balance online and make sure there are no irregular charges pending. We were able to call our bank, have the charges blocked, and have new cards sent to us without a problem. For this reason, we highly recommend you have multiple cards for your primary bank account.

Exchanging Currency

It's always best to avoid changing large amounts of cash at borders. With the exception of the Costa Rica/Panama border, money changers have approached us at every crossing. The guys with the fanny-packs and fat stacks of cash will take you for 5-10%. As a rule of thumb, exchange rates from border changers are usually better in the country you are entering, rather than the country you are leaving. Banks will always have a better rate than border changers, but not all banks offer the service.

Always know the exchange rate of the country you're entering before you reach the border to keep from being ripped off. Use XE for up-to-date rates, no matter how new your guidebook is. Don't be afraid to haggle over the rate and bring a calculator unless you're good at quickly dividing by decimals in your head.

US dollars seem to be widely accepted in many Central American countries and some areas of Mexico, especially touristy places. El Salvador and Panama both use the dollar as their currency and most places we went in Costa Rica freely accepted US bills at a decent exchange rate.

How We Manage Money

We have personal checking accounts with Charles Schwab, one of the best banks to use for long-term travel due low ATM fees. We also have online savings accounts with ING Direct that are connected to our Charles Schwab account and our personal checking accounts with the brick and mortar banks we use back home.

Savings Accounts

ING allows us to accrue better-than-average interest and easily transfer money between our accounts back home and our travel checking accounts with Schwab. It is safer to keep a low balance in your primary checking account and periodically transfer money into it from a second account. Although your bank usually reverses fraudulent charges, it can take time and may put your money in limbo for a while.

Shared Checking Accounts

The three of us also have a shared checking account with Charles Schwab that we use for group expenses such as food, lodging and gas. Every two or three months we transfer money from our ING savings accounts to the shared account to cover the next leg of our trip.

This is only necessary because there are three of us, and only two are married to each other. Regardless, if more than person is going on this trip, it's a good idea to have a shared account just in case. The extra ATM card may come in handy, and having two names on the account means either of you can talk to the bank if something happens.

Cash on Hand

We withdraw three to five days worth of cash at a time, usually $200 to $400. The bulk of that money stays locked in our car, and the rest, usually around $100, stays with us in a wallet.

We've found from previous trips that it's helpful to think of your cash withdraws as "days worth of money". The easiest way to stay on target is to consistently keep daily expenses within the planned amount. If you have a pile of cash that's supposed to last three days, make it last three days. It's much harder to keep track of what you spend if you are constantly running to the ATM or using plastic for purchases.

We also keep a stash of a couple hundred dollars hidden in our car in case of emergency. It's a good safety net if the only ATM in town is out of service or we come up short at a border crossing.

13

Food

We have certainly not starved on this trip.

Buying food, cooking it, and eating out is a daily experience that gets a bit more interesting once you cross into Mexico. It's a cultural adventure that never ceases, and changes with each country.

Food is one of the most enjoyable aspects of this trip, but it can also be frustrating and time consuming. It takes time to figure out the best ways to feed yourself while constantly on the move. Not to mention how to use ingredients you aren't familiar with, and how to order off a menu you probably don't understand.

We cook the vast majority of our meals. Partially out of necessity, but mostly because it's the best way to save money. We often find ourselves in remote locations with very limited options for grabbing a bite to eat. Thanks to our fridge, we're able to stock up on groceries for three or four days and hit the road without worries. If we didn't have the fridge or the means to cook, finding three square meals a day would be a constant hassle.

Eating out is something we do more out of convenience than necessity. We almost always cook breakfast and dinner, and stop for lunch or snacks when the mood hits us. The food in Mexico and Central America is amazing. The typical staples, corn tortillas, rice, beans and plantains are simple, but almost always well prepared. Small stands and restaurants are cheap and full of delicious local eats. We have certainly not starved on this trip.

Buying Groceries

Supermarkets can be found in every decent-sized town. They aren't always up to US standards, but they have enough variety and products you will recognize that sorting out a few meals isn't a problem. It's not something we're proud of, but we've been to no less than four Walmarts since entering Mexico. Back home we would tend to avoid giant chain grocery stories. On the road we look forward to the convenience, and being able to stock up on harder to find staples that smaller markets don't carry.

The quality and value of grocery stores throughout Mexico and Central America varies greatly. Some only carry only non-perishable and frozen food, others rival the best upscale supermarkets in the US. As a rule of thumb, the bigger the city, the more likely you are to find fancy grocery stores. The smaller the town, the more likely you are to find cheaper grocery stores with less variety.

+ FOR MORE INFO SEARCH LIFEREMOTELY.COM

Tips for the Traveling Camp Chef

Belize and Guatemala were the two countries where we had a hard time finding larger, well-stocked stores. El Salvador, especially the capital San Salvador, and Costa Rica had the greatest variety. Our vote for the best supermarkets goes to Mexico. The variety of baked goods in big Mexican grocery stores is unbelievable. Plus, they carry plenty of imported foods from up north, helping to ease you into grocery shopping south of the border.

The further we traveled into Central America the more comfortable we got with buying meat from the butcher, produce from the street-side stand, and bread from the baker. It takes a bit more planning and decent Spanish skills, but it's always cheaper and often a better product than big supermarkets.

Finding El Supermercado

Your best bet for finding a big supermarket is to look just outside town on major highways. There are usually two or three companies prevalent in each country. Once you know what to ask for and what the sign looks like, it's a piece of cake to find a store. Lonely Planet guides and Google Maps may help you find groceries in a specific city, although they rarely mention every option available.

In smaller towns about all you can do is drive around looking out the window, or stop and ask someone where to find "el supermercado". The going gets a bit tougher in rural areas. Small roadside shops are everywhere, but the selection of meats and produce may be limited to processed ham and a bunch of plantains. Good in a pinch, but not helpful if you want to stock up on three days of balanced meals.

Markets

Markets are another source for buying groceries. You have to be a bit more adventurous to wander through the crowded, smelly, labyrinthine corridors of an open-air market, but that's half the fun. Markets are a great place to see local culture at its best, and to sample and purchase the tastiest, freshest food a country has to offer.

Most decent-sized towns have a designated central market area. The largest and most intimidating occurring in big cities where you can buy anything imaginable, provided you can find and recognize it.

We tend to frequent markets as tourists rather than shoppers. It's easy to grab a few snacks and fresh produce, but shopping for several days of full meals in a crowded and unfamiliar market is a time-consuming task.

The market in Antigua, Guatemala.

Cooking Food

We eat well, mostly because we cook for ourselves at every given opportunity. Not to say you can't get great food at the restaurant down the street, we simply prefer the convenience and cost-effectiveness of doing it ourselves.

Use Local Ingredients

The key is to add variety. Don't constrain yourself to what you are used to eating back home. Learn how the locals do it and mix up your meals with flavors and ingredients you can't find back home. Easier said than done, we certainly still struggle with it, but learning to incorporate new local ingredients is the best way to eat well and add variety to your diet.

The staples of Latin American cooking are rice, beans, tortillas and plantains. Add a bit of chicken, beef or fish and you've got a $1.50 meal that's guaranteed to fill you up. Fresh produce (especially tropical fruits) are your best bet for cheap and delicious meals. Mangos, papayas, oranges, and bananas can be had for next to nothing at roadside stands and open-air markets. Produce you've never heard of starts popping up once you hit southern Mexico. Once you know what to look for and how to prepare it you're in for a treat.

Making friends is the best way to sort out the complexities of unknown ingredients. For us, one of the best parts of our homestay and language lessons in Guatemala was learning what people eat and how to prepare local ingredients. Paying for cooking classes is also a fantastic (but pricey) way to learn about local foods and ingredients. We took a class in Oaxaca, Mexico that taught us a couple easy dishes that we cook regularly on the road, and a few fancy ones we can use to impress our friends back home.

Stoves & Grills

For most of this trip we cooked on two small multi-fuel backpacking stoves. Finding fuel for the stoves was easy, although locating white gas, our fuel of choice, became more difficult once we entered Central America. In Mexico it's easy to buy it at the paint store chain called Comex. However every Comex store we asked in Central America did not carry white gas. Alternative fuels such as kerosene, diesel and gas (petrol) are available everywhere.

In Panama we picked up a two burner Coleman propane stove. It uses small one-pound green bottles that can be found in large hardware stores throughout most of Latin America. Our plan is to purchase an adapter for our stove and a larger refillable tank in South America.

Using propane to cook is a common choice among overlanders. Filling a propane tank can be a chore in some countries, but it is more convenient for cooking. It can take a few minutes to start a backpacking stove that runs on liquid fuel, and regulating the heat on some models is dicey business. If we had to do it again, we would have brought a multi-fuel stove that could be instantly lit and finely adjusted. Assuming such a thing exists.

Grilling is another cooking method we use frequently. It's a great way to add a lot more variety to your meal plan. If you have the space and are already lugging around a propane tank, a small collapsible gas grill isn't a bad idea. We opted for a folding metal grill rack that we use on charcoal fires. It's a bit more hassle than cooking on gas, but charcoal is cheap and available everywhere.

Eating Out

Local eateries are everywhere. Most offer a set, or very limited menu. With few exceptions the food is simple, cheap, and delicious. In poorer Central American countries meals can be had for $2-3. In parts of Mexico, Costa

Rica and Panama the prices are a bit higher, $5 or more. A typical set meal includes your choice of meat, rice, beans, plantains, and sometimes cheese, fresh fruit or veggies.

Street vendors and snack stalls are great places to stop for lunch or a quick bite to eat. Tacos, tostadas, fried plantains, tamales, and grilled meats are always a winner. In Mexico, look for places that sell "antojitos"; there you'll find all of your favorite Mexican snacks, done right. In Central America look for restaurants with signs saying comedor, pupuseria, comida rapida, or comida corriente. Don't expect a fancy restaurant, just good cheap local food.

Tourist restaurants should be avoided, especially those setup on major highways that service tour buses. You can usually recognize them because they are surrounded by souvenir shops and are devoid of customers unless there's a bus parked out front. If you're in a Spanish-speaking country and the menus are in English, or if you're outside of Panama or El Salvador and prices are in US dollars, find someplace else to eat.

Street meat in Juayua, El Salvador during the weekend Feria Gastronómica.

14

Safety

Although the crime situation in Mexico and Central America is often sensationalized (thanks Fox News), it is still a very real problem. Just like the crime in Detroit, Brooklyn and nearby our old house on South Jackson Street in Seattle.

People are generally friendly and polite, they want to help you, not rob you. Unfortunately every place in the world has its share of sleaze balls that are going to try to take advantage of you. Put your smart hat on, trust your intuition, and for goodness sake, practice using that amazing thing called common sense.

When in doubt, talk to locals. Hotel receptionists, shop owners, and police officers know their town best. For the most part they want to help you because they benefit more from your safety. Taking two minutes to ask if parking, walking or sleeping in a place is safe may save you a world of trouble later.

Safety Tips

- Do not drive at night. I repeat, do not drive at night. Not so much out of fear of being robbed, but because of bad road conditions, pedestrians, animals, and the difficulty of navigating.
- Always be alert of your surroundings. If it feels wrong, leave. This goes for anywhere, including your backyard.
- Ask a local for up-to-date information if you have doubts about a place, or have heard of a history of problems in the area. Uniformed police and military can be helpful in this regard.
- Check online for up-to-date travel advisories.
- Be prudent when handing over important paperwork such your driver's license and passport. Never let them out of your sight.

- Don't look like a rich tourist. The more expensive clothing, jewelry and camera equipment you show off, the bigger the target you are.
- Don't camp or boondock alone. Don't pitch a tent or park your rig where there are no other people. Don't be alone on a beach. If you sleep in your vehicle, think about leaving your keys in the ignition in case you need to jet in a hurry.
- Carry a cell phone. Know the emergency numbers for the country you are in.
- Don't get drunk and stumble home. Actually, it's best if you don't get drunk at all unless you have someone to babysit you.
- Petty theft is by far the most likely crime you could be the victim of. Keep your stuff locked up and out of sight. Watch your wallet in crowded places. Pay closer attention to what's going on in tourist areas, they tend to attract the most thieves.

15

Driving

Road Conditions

Road conditions in Latin America run the gamut from bad to worse, with a few exceptions. Toll roads in Mexico are comparable to US freeways. Highways in Central American countries tend to be a step below the worst two-lane roads you'd encounter in the States.

If you are lucky enough to find yourself on a newly constructed road, expect smooth sailing. However, the methods used to build and repair roads don't usually make a lot of sense. The road could be beautiful flat tarmac for twenty miles, and then turn into a pothole-filled obstacle course, followed by a dirt path to nowhere.

The vast majority of the ground we covered in Mexico and Central America was on two-lane roads with no shoulder. Generally, the best highways in Central America can be found in Costa Rica and Panama.

The four-lane highway after crossing the border into Panama, a rare sight in Central America.

The Pan-American is, at minimum, a paved two-lane highway for the entire stretch to Panama, although the conditions vary widely.

Major roads around large cities, especially Central American capitals, tend to be in decent shape and may even be four-lane divided highways. But that doesn't mean they won't be packed full of busses, semi-trucks, farm animals, student drivers and police checkpoints. Deviating far from the Pan-American, especially in rural areas, is always a gamble.

What to Watch Out For

In most cases roads lack sidewalks. Major highways pass straight through towns without thought to how on-ramps, off-ramps, or pedestrian crossings should be built. Speed bumps, potholes, missing manhole covers and half-completed construction zones appear out of nowhere. Cars share the road with bicycles, motorcycles, livestock, trucks that move at a snail's pace, and vehicles that would never pass inspection back in the States.

All of these obstacles can combine to make for very stressful driving conditions. It's not all bad. It's part of the adventure. However, for your own safety and for the wellbeing of your vehicle, it's crucial that you pay very close attention while driving in Latin America.

Because of the multitude of obstacles, and the difficulty you may have seeing them even in broad daylight, avoid driving at night.

Speed Bumps

Speed bumps are especially common in Mexico on non-toll roads. There rarely seems to be a rhyme or reason to speed bump placement, size or visibility. In many places it appears as if people build their own speed bumps in front of shops or roadside stands to force drivers to slow down and check out their goods.

When you're in speed bump country, drive slowly, and always watch the road. Don't expect the speed bump to be painted, or to see a sign. If you want to avoid the topes in Mexico, shell out the cash for the toll road. It saves you from potential car repairs down the road and halves your drive time.

In Central American countries the speed bumps calm down a bit, and you start to notice a few patterns. They appear when entering small towns, where buildings are close to the road, and in front of bus stops, schools, and police stations. Don't get too comfortable though, you never know what's around the next corner.

Road Construction

If you see a guy wearing orange, or at least holding a flag, or maybe a red t-shirt, you've found the road construction. If he's holding a flag in front of himself, or waving it up and down with both hands, you should stop and put on your hazard lights for the drivers behind you.

Rather than build one stretch at a time, it's common to find highways ripped up for miles, with work being done sporadically in different areas. Lane swapping and driving on shoulders or improvised dirt roads is commonplace in construction zones and can go on for many miles.

It helps to ask around about road conditions if you have more than one option or are on a tight schedule. Construction can quickly turn the nicest-looking road on the map into a six-hour stop-and-go dustbowl.

Potholes

Major highways in most countries tend to be relatively flat, with the worst conditions being in Honduras, Guatemala and Nicaragua. Roads in the rest of the countries tend to be patched frequently, which doesn't exactly make for a smooth drive, but at least you aren't zigzagging your way across two lanes and the shoulder to avoid snapping an axle.

Once you leave the main thoroughfares it gets a bit more interesting. Potholes are frequently filled with dirt or gravel, which often does more harm than good. Again, our advice is to slow down and keep a sharp eye out for craters.

Pedestrians & Animals

Sidewalks in small towns and rural communities are not very well developed. Typically people either walk in the road, or on small dirt paths just off the shoulder. Given that there are rarely shoulders on the road, you will frequently find yourself driving very close to pedestrians. A horn honk is a good idea if they are facing the other way and may not hear you coming.

Animals, on the other hand, don't always respond to blaring horns. Dogs are the biggest problem. They have a tendency to lie in the middle of the road, rarely bothering to move as you approach. Sadly, dead and horribly maimed stray dogs are a common sight from Mexico south. We've come across plenty of cows, horses and chickens in the road as well. Unlike dogs, they're usually smart enough to get out of the way when they see a car approaching.

Road Signs & Getting Directions

Unless your Spanish is decent, it's a good idea to keep a dictionary in the car as you head into Mexico. Road signs are always written in Spanish and there may not be symbols or pictures to give you an idea of the meaning. Church's RV and campground book has a cheat sheet with translated road signs that we found invaluable until our Spanish improved.

Another type of "road sign" you'll encounter consists of rocks or tree branches in the road. This is a Latin American warning triangle. It signifies that a vehicle, road slide, or other obstruction is blocking the lane up ahead. Proceed with caution.

"The road is in a bad state", near Santa Elena, Costa Rica.

Signs for highways and city streets are usually inaccurate or non-existent. There are exceptions, but it can be difficult to find your way without a good map, GPS, or stopping to ask for directions. Deciphering directions can be an exercise in futility, even if your Spanish is good.

Due to the lack of addresses and street signs, verbal directions typically involve landmarks and other obscure references that never fail to confuse. In our experience, if the directions were more complicated than "straight ahead, blue building on the left," we'd have to stop again and ask someone else. Only to receive directions that were totally different than what the first guy said. Our most successful experiences were using a pen and paper, or talking in front of a paper or GPS map.

Note that in Spanish the word for straight is derecho and the word for right is derecha. Confusing the two will either lead to driving in circles or heading straight out of town. Thankfully the word for left is unmistakably izquierda.

Slow Moving Vehicles

Big trucks and underpowered cars are commonplace on roads in Mexico and Central America. You'll encounter them everywhere, especially while climbing hills. The rules for passing are the same as in the US: don't cross the solid yellow line. However, in many cases there are no lines, or the guys who painted the lines didn't bother to add dashed lines to straight, flat sections for passing. In any case, drivers tend to ignore lines on the road, opting to use their intuition to choose the best time to pass.

When approaching a slow vehicle, turn on your hazards to warn cars behind you. If the driver signals with his left indicator, he may be giving you the thumbs up to pass. If he does this while braking or waving his arm out the window, he's probably about to turn left.

Before attempting to pass a slow vehicle check behind you and make sure someone else doesn't have the same idea. If you act defensively, other drivers may become impatient and take matters into their own hands. If someone behind or in front of you is starting to pass, let him go and make sure there's enough room in front of your car so that he can get back into the lane if vehicles approach from the other direction.

Dirt Roads

If the road turns to dirt, you're in for fun times. Sometimes highways will turn to dirt for short stretches, which is usually nothing to worry about provided you drive slowly. If you know you are going to be driving on a dirt road, make sure your car can handle it. We've driven on some very gnarly roads, especially in Costa Rica, but we knew what we were getting ourselves into and had a 4x4 and recovery gear to get us through it.

In the rainy season dirt roads can quickly become impassable. Washouts and landslides can seasonally close some roads for weeks or months. If in doubt, ask around about current road conditions. Your ability to make it through can change overnight.

Off-roading in Costa Rica around Lake Arenal.

River Crossings

Driving off-road, or down dirt roads out in the bush may require getting a little wet. Here are a few tips to make help you make it safely across water features:

- Walk it first. If you can't walk it, don't drive it. Check the depth, current, hardness of the ground and look for any hidden obstacles such as boulders and submerged logs.

- Make sure your vehicle can handle it. 4x4 and enough clearance to keep the battery, harness, and most importantly the engine air intake above the water. Check with your vehicle's manufacturer or ask advice on overlanding or 4x4 forums.

- For deep crossings you may need to install a snorkel and other waterproofing modifications to keep from doing harm to your vehicle.
- Keep the windows down in case the car stalls or the electrics short and you need to bail out.
- Let the car cool down before entering the water. Cold water can warp hot brake rotors and damage the catalytic converter.
- Turn off your headlights and check for water before turning them back on.
- Check the entry and exit points, they can be steep, washed out, and may prove to be the most difficult parts of the crossing.
- Make sure you're in low-range four-wheel drive. Keep it in first or second gear and do not shift during the crossing.

Crossing a river in Costa Rica near El Castillo.

- Drive slowly into and through the water. If water crests the hood, you are driving too fast.
- Keep light pressure on the gas to keep water out of your exhaust and to avoid stalling.
- If you do stall, you may not be able to start again. If the tailpipe or airbox is under water, do not attempt to restart your car. This may cause hydro-lock, which is a great way to destroy an engine. Exit your vehicle down-stream to avoid being sucked under your car, and winch or tow yourself out.
- Check your axle, transmission and differential oil after crossing. Water may have come in during the crossing.
- If you crossed through salt water, hose off the engine bay and undercarriage as soon as possible to prevent corrosion.
- Be extra careful during the rainy season. Crossings may be small trickles one moment, and raging torrents the next. We've passed through ankle-deep creeks, only to return three days later to find water above our waist.

Police & Military Checkpoints

Checkpoints are commonplace throughout Mexico and Central America. Many are impromptu police checkpoints; others are permanent installations operated by the military between state borders. In every case the officials are looking for contraband, primarily drugs, weapons, and illegal immigrants.

Keep a calm head, smile, be friendly and make small talk. Even though they may be touting decommissioned US Army semiautomatic rifles, these guys are just doing their job, which is to make the country safer for everyone. Give them what they want, keep an eye on your car and paperwork, and chances are you'll be on your way in less than five minutes.

> Even though they may be touting decommissioned US Army semiautomatic rifles, these guys are just doing their job, which is to make the country safer for everyone.

We were stopped a number of times in Mexico, especially on the Baja peninsula and in the southern states where the left-wing Zapatista movement is still active. In Central America we were stopped in every country at least once. The vast majority of checkpoints were nothing more than two-minute inconveniences. 90% of the time we were simply waved through with a nod and a smile. The rest of the time we were asked to provide a license or passport and the vehicle's paperwork before being allowed to proceed. In total, our car has been looked over three times, once by a dog, but never thoroughly searched.

Police Corruption

Bribery attempts are frequently reported in Latin America. Many countries have come a long way with cleaning up their police forces and corruption is much less common than it used to be. We have never had a problem on this trip, although we've heard a few first-hand reports from friends. We have dealt with our fair share of police corruption in Africa, so we entered Latin America knowing what to look out for.

Methods for dealing with bribery attempts vary, depending on your attitude and how big of a hurry you are in. Most people prefer to stick it out as long as possible and feel that handing over money will only make the problem worse for others. We tend to agree, with a few exceptions.

A police officer should never ask for money. In most countries it is illegal and fines must be paid at a police station or bank. Bribe shakedowns typically start after you've been stopped and cited for a bogus infraction. The cop will tell you what you have to do to pay the (usually outrageous) fine. This often involves driving an hour in the wrong direction to a police station. As soon as you decline, he'll offer a cheaper alternative, cash in his hand.

If you sense a bribe attempt coming, be very careful handing over original paperwork. Keep copies or old expired IDs handy. An international driver's license is particularly useful in this case. The only sure way for a corrupt cop to get your money is if he's holding something you need. If he is very insistent upon seeing your original documents, offer to follow him to the police station to take care of business. It's not likely he'll get a bribe out of you at the police station, so he might decline the request.

You have three options for a persistent cop, either call his bluff, politely stand your ground, or play dumb. If you happily agree to his original request and offer to drive hour out of the way to pay a fine, he might lose interest. Acting like you don't know any Spanish is a good way to start. Speak in a language other than English if you can. We've met plenty of police officers that could understand and speak a bit of English.

The general consensus is that the best way to get out of a bribe is to use a variety of techniques to waste his time more than he's wasting yours. Stay happy and smiley, play dumb, nod and agree, but do nothing. Let him get frustrated and leave once he realizes you aren't going to pay him.

If you're left with a persistent cop and are short on time, the only option may be to pay what he's asking. We believe this is a last resort. Paying bribes does not improve the situation for future travelers.

16

The Language Barrier

Traveling in Latin America with a limited knowledge of Spanish is a difficult endeavor. It is doable, but you will have a much more enjoyable time if you take the time to pick up the language. Spanish is not difficult to learn, there are thousands of words shared between it and English.

Our knowledge of Spanish was pretty close to zero when we started planning for this trip. We managed to do a bit of self-studying before hitting the road, and listened to a few audio lessons while driving south. Add in a bit of dictionary diving and online translating and we made it through Mexico, barely. It wasn't always fun, and we would have gotten much more out of it if we had done a better job with the lessons before leaving home.

In Guatemala we stopped to take lessons and live with a local family for seven weeks. In that time we gained more than enough Spanish skills to be comfortable traveling and conversing in simple situations. Our ability to get advice from locals, bargain for deals, and find what we needed increased tenfold. The trip became a whole new experience.

In parts of Mexico, Costa Rica, Panama and all of Belize you will find English speakers. Big urban centers and tourist towns tend to have more than most. Hostels and tour companies operated by expats are also likely to have more than one person you can easily converse with. We've also found that if the place has a decent-looking web page in English, chances are you'll find it spoken there.

The Bare Essentials

We're not here to teach you Spanish; you'll have to figure that part out for yourself. To illustrate what you should know, we've provided a list of common situations you will encounter from the day you cross into Mexico.

- How to say you can't speak Spanish very well.
- How to say thank you, you're welcome, sorry and pardon me.
- How to politely ask the person talking to speak more slowly.
- How to get gas at a full-service station.
- How to find the banjercito (the bank/vehicle permit facility) at the border crossing into Mexico.
- How to find a campsite, ask how much it costs, and where to find water, power, bathrooms and showers.
- How to make a hotel reservation, and what to do when you get there.
- How to ask for and understand driving directions. Good luck!
- How to order food and drinks at a restaurant or bar.

When in doubt, ask yes or no questions!

- How to buy meat at a butcher and veggies at a produce stand.
- How to get a haircut.
- How to buy a SIM card for a phone, and add time to a prepaid plan.
- How to ask for the password for a wifi connection.
- How to handle border crossings. Including immigration, customs, fumigation, inspections, and changing money.
- How to handle police checkpoints. How to explain where you came from, where you are going, and what you are doing in the country.

Self-Studying

Before we left home we spent some time perusing phrase books and trying to learn the basics. Our efforts were largely unsuccessful. Planning and preparing for this trip, while simultaneously working, moving, and dealing with the five thousand little chores in between took up all of our time. If we were to do it again, our best bet may have been to enroll in language classes at a local school, or arrange a private tutor for the three of us.

Audio lessons are a great way to pick up a bit of Spanish while you're driving.

That said, we did try our hand at self-studying. We followed Rosetta Stone through a couple units, and found audio lessons that came in handy once we started driving. Rosetta Stone might have worked had we started it sooner and had more time closer to our departure date. It's a difficult way to learn practical information quickly. And it requires a lot of focus and the patience to backtrack once you've gone too far or spent too long without studying.

Audio lessons are a great way to pick up a bit of Spanish while you're driving. We can highly recommend the Pimsleur series. It's repetitive enough that you can follow along while focusing on the road, and starts off with words and phrases that are immediately useful. Each lesson lasts about 30 minutes and involves a lot of "repeat after me" or "how do you say…" Without a doubt, we learned more useful words and phrases from Pimsleur than we did from Rosetta Stone.

Regardless, our efforts at learning Spanish on our own were a resounding failure compared to what we learned in a single week of one-on-one Spanish lessons in Guatemala. Talking to a native speaker and using the language every day, for every task, is by far the most efficient way to learn. No magical computer programs or audio lessons will be able to do a better job.

Spanish Lessons and Homestays

Stopping in Mexico or Guatemala to learn Spanish, or to brush up on your antiquated high-school lessons, is a fantastic idea. It may cost a chunk of change, but it will make the rest of your trip much more enjoyable. Guatemala is a common choice. In Mexico prices tend to be slightly higher, and English is more commonly spoken, making travel through the area easier.

Prices in Guatemala are around $4-5 per hour, and get lower depending on how many hours you sign up for. We'd recommend a minimum of three weeks. We opted for six, but honestly could have done with fewer lessons and more real-life practice. You can only absorb so many verb tenses before they start to blend together.

One-on-one lessons are worth the extra cost. Everyone learns differently. We got the most out of simply speaking with our teachers. Having structured lessons and learning grammar was helpful, but the most useful part is talking to a native speaker who is patient and will correct your mistakes.

Us with our Guatemalan Spanish teachers in Antigua.

Our language classes included field trips, educational videos, and a few games of Spanish Scrabble. They were also a fantastic way to learn about special events happening around town. We took a trip to the central market with our teachers, visited several churches, and learned about the Semana Santa (Lent and Easter) celebrations in the city. Our classes were enriching in more ways than just learning the language.

Antigua, Xela and San Pedro La Laguna in Guatemala are common places for combining one-on-one language lessons with a homestay. We highly recommend coupling Spanish lessons with a homestay. Not only will it force you to practice your Spanish, you will learn a massive amount about local culture.

Most homestays can be arranged to include food, and are priced very reasonably. We paid $75 per person, per week for our homestay. It included three delicious meals cooked by our host mother every day of the week except Sunday. Our language school, La Union, is based in Antigua and cost $100 per person per week for 20 hours of lessons. In the afternoons we volunteered for Global Visionaries, which gave our brains a rest from the morning's class. Combining homestay, volunteering and Spanish school made for full days, but it was without a doubt one of the best experiences we've had on the trip.

Our classes were enriching in more ways than just learning the language.

17

Staying Connected

Friends, family, and online followers all demand that you stay in touch. For us the biggest challenge is staying connected with our clients back home. We work ten to fifteen hours each week and go to extreme lengths to assure we have regular internet access and phone reception. We're solidly on the internet-addicted side of the fence.

FOR MORE INFO SEARCH LIFEREMOTELY.COM

How to Find Internet Access Anywhere in the World

Aside from our 15-hour per week work commitments, we see our technological toys as simply another tool in the toolbox. They keep us safer, more informed, and help us plan our travels.

Easy access to the internet is the best means for researching destinations, finding and reserving hotels, navigating to the next stop, and diagnosing problems with our vehicle or gear. We can't count the number of times we've avoided hassles by being able to be online at a moment's notice.

General Connection Availability

In the US and Canada getting online is no problem. High-speed wifi connections are everywhere. Mobile network carriers offer prepaid plans for phones and internet. Although they are relatively expensive, they tend to work every place you'd expect: major highways, cities, and most smaller towns. Bandwidth is decent and 3G coverage is increasing every day. Internet cafés, coffee shops and free wifi in chain stores such as McDonalds, Starbucks and libraries make it easy to find a connection.

You do not, under any circumstance, want to travel internationally with your domestic cell phone contract. The international data roaming fee for major US carriers is $20 per megabyte. If you have an unlocked phone that uses GSM (SIM cards), it's worth bringing it with and purchasing local prepaid plans in countries you visit. It still may be worth bringing along a locked phone to use when you can connect to a wireless signal. We have one of each. Our unlocked phone sees lots of use, the other hasn't been touched since we left the USA.

You do not, under any circumstance, want to travel internationally with your domestic cell phone contract.

In Mexico and Central America connectivity gets a bit more interesting. Internet cafés are still abundant, but they aren't always the most comfortable places to spend an afternoon. Prices are generally one to two dollars per hour. Coffee shops, restaurants and hotels readily advertise free wifi, although it's not something you can count on seeing everywhere. If you need internet at the next stop, verify that it's available. Don't expect to show up at a hostel and have online access. You can find more detailed information on connectivity in Part 3.

Connection Speed and Reliability

Internet speed and reliability in Latin America is hit or miss. We've had countless problems staying connected and finding enough bandwidth for big downloads. Poor infrastructure, power outages, and fickle wireless routers are usually to blame. There's absolutely no way to know what the speed and reliability of a given connection may be like. We've had awesome internet in $5 campsites, and horrendous connections in $40 hotel rooms.

On the other hand, cell phone reception tends to be very good, especially in poorer countries that lack landline infrastructure. For example, if you look at the 3G availability map for Guatemala you will have a hard time finding a populated area that does not have coverage. The increased availability of high-speed cell networks make 3G USB modems and excellent way to stay connected.

Useful Gear

The big three: a laptop, an unlocked 3G USB modem (aka a dongle) and an unlocked quad-band GSM phone. With all of these devices, you can have internet and make phone calls just about anywhere you go.

It is possible to forego the 3G modem in exchange for tethering your cell phone and laptop. It's also possible to make calls using VOIP programs such as Skype or Google Talk instead of with a cell phone. We had to rule these options out due to our work commitments and our less-than-stellar experiences with tethering and VOIP. In our experience, internet connections were too unreliable for weekly phone calls.

A wireless router and wireless extender cards for our laptops are two other pieces of gear we've found very useful. We can plug our 3G modem into the router, allowing us to share the connection on multiple laptops. Not a necessity for most people, we use it when the three of us are holed up for a workday in a place without wifi.

FOR MORE INFO SEARCH LIFEREMOTELY.COM

Wireless Data Access via a Phone, Dongle or Mobile Hotspot

How to Choose an International Mobile Phone

Wireless extenders serve two purposes. They let us reach signals at a greater distance and act as a backup in case our laptop's internal wireless cards don't play nice with the router. The latter is a problem we've experienced frequently. It's common that two of us can get online fine, and the third, for some unexplained reason, cannot.

A 3G-enabled Kindle is another good addition to your gear. Aside from using it to read books, it will get you online for free in every country except Belize and Costa Rica. It works great for emailing and Googling, but the browser won't support more complex tasks.

Phone & 3G Modem Setup

Prepaid phones and 3G modems need to be setup in every country you visit. After going through this process seven or eight times we've become fairly proficient at it. It's not always easy, and knowledgeable salesmen can be hard to come by. It helps if you understand the process before showing up at the store.

The typical process for setting up a phone:

1. Locate a store that sells SIM cards. They are everywhere. Once you are familiar with the popular cell phone company logos (Telcel, Tigo, Movistar and Claro to name the most common) it's easy to spot places where you can recharge or buy SIM cards. See our phone reports in Part 3 for company listings.
2. Buy a SIM card. They usually only cost a couple dollars. If they won't sell it to you because you are a foreigner, go down to the street to a place that will. We had this happen once in El Salvador and have heard of it happening to travelers in other countries.
3. Make sure the store activates the SIM card. That usually involves the clerk making a call and/or putting the SIM in his phone and pushing some magic buttons. This typically takes five or ten minutes.
4. The SIM will come with a phone number and a pin number. Do not lose either of these. You will need the phone number to recharge, and the pin number the first time you put the SIM in your phone.
5. Add money to your prepaid account. This typically involves giving the nice person your phone number, and handing over some cash. The amount is up to you. Sometimes it is in fixed increments, and sometimes you have to buy recharge cards that you activate yourself from the phone. Once recharged, you should immediately receive a text message saying money has been added to your balance.

Checking Your Balance and Recharging

Finding out your available balance can be tricky until you know what to ask for. "Saldo" is the word you want, and typically you get it by sending a text to a number. Ask the person who sets up your SIM card for this information, it will be different for every country and provider.

To add more time to your cell phone, find a place that offers "recarga" (recharge) for your brand of SIM. This has always been a simple process, and can be done everywhere. Keep an eye out for special promotions. "Triple saldo" in Mexico and Guatemala gave us three dollars balance for every one we paid. In El Salvador we found that we could use Claro to call the US for 30 minutes at a price of $0.75 by calling a number and activating a special plan. If you call internationally frequently these promotions can save you a lot of money.

See our Country Information sections in Part 3 for more information about country-specific wireless, phone, and internet reports with prices, setup instructions, and availability.

Using Data on Your Smartphone and Unlocked USB Modems

Activating data on the phone involves sending a text to a special number, usually with a message stating the amount of time you want, "hora" for an hour, "dia" for a day, "semana" for a week, etc. The number, message, and available time increments varies by provider and country.

Once you have data activated you can move the SIM card to an unlocked 3G modem. With some modems you are able to send text messages directly. This saves you from having to move the SIM between your phone and modem every time you need to activate more data.

Depending on your modem and how old the software is, you might need to create a profile and enter some information before it will work. The magical information you need is called an APN; it changes in each country and for each cell company. You may need more settings than just the APN, but all of this information is easy to find online. Our experiences finding people who could answer our questions were mixed. Your best bet will be in big stores that sell 3G modems and are owned and operated by a cell company.

Prepaid USB Modems

If you plan to stay in one country for a while, it may be cheaper and easier to buy a prepaid modem that is locked to a specific company instead of using an unlocked modem. Some companies offer modems for around $25 and include up to a month of free time. We bought modems in Mexico, Guatemala, El Salvador and Nicaragua, and used our unlocked modem everywhere else.

18

Working on the Road

We each spend an average of 15 hours per week working on the road. Our goal is to offset the cost of the trip by earning money from clients in the US while we travel. We're called digital nomads or location independent professionals. It's a growing trend, made possible by the internet, and is a fantastic way to pay the bills while traveling. For the most part this has been a success. But it has affected how we travel, and certainly does not make life easier.

Jessica is a freelance graphic designer, Kobus teaches online and builds web sites, and Jared is a software developer. We can work anywhere that has internet and a cell phone signal. We have designated work days every Tuesday, no matter where we are, how hot it is, or how hungover we are.

FOR MORE INFO SEARCH LIFEREMOTELY.COM

Getting Started

Freelancing

Telecommuting

Staying Connected

Online Tools

A work day means we don't go anywhere. We find a good campground or hostel with internet and we stay put. We arrive the day before and stay the night after. Having a specific day helps us set a schedule and plan around our travels. It also tells our clients when we'll be online, and when we are available to do work. Here are a few pros and cons if you're thinking of taking your job with you on the Pan-Am:

Pros

- First world income, third world expenses. In other words, we can work two days a week and pay all of our bills.
- We don't have to burn any bridges or lose every client. When we stop traveling we'll have a source of income when we get home.
- No gaps in the resume, and we stay on top of the changes in our field making us more employable if we need to look for full-time work.

- No need to save for years before leaving on a trip.
- We can continue to travel as long as we have work.

Cons

READ MORE

For more info about becoming a digital nomad, or what it's like to work while traveling, see our website.

- Trips that involve a lot of moving around (like this one) are invariably affected by our need to work. We have to plan our travels around when we need to work, making us less flexible.
- We're reliant on having internet and power for work days. And we need intermittent connectivity throughout the week to check emails.
- Bad internet or power outages can mean we have to move, head into town to find a café, or postpone work.
- Finding a quiet and peaceful place can be difficult, especially if you need to make a phone call.
- Being disciplined can be tough. It's not easy to sit on a white sandy beach all day in front of a laptop.

19

Accommodation

Finding cheap places to say and cooking your own meals are the two best ways to save money on this trip. Most overlanders choose to camp to save money, and because it's often the most comfortable option available. If you can sleep in your vehicle, it's not difficult to find free or very cheap places to park for the night. We tent camp. Because of this we have spent very few nights camping for free. To us, finding and paying for an established camping spot is worth the added effort.

Cheap hotels and hostels are the budget-minded alternative to camping. Finding a place with secured parking is the biggest concern. This can be difficult in big cities where it's common to be forced to stay in a hotel due to a lack of camping options. We sometimes end up paying more for a hotel with parking because we aren't comfortable leaving our car on the street.

Hostels tend to have more services and a variety of accommodation options to fit your budget. Most have a kitchen, or at least a cheap restaurant. Hostels are a great place to meet people, and are usually a much more enjoyable place to spend time than a budget hotel. The downside is that they can be noisier, and may attract a type of crowd (rowdy college spring-breakers for example) that may not be to your liking. If you've done any backpacking, you'll know exactly what to expect.

We will gladly pay $15 extra for a hotel or hostel that has a kitchen or allows us to cook with our own gear. The cost to eat in a restaurant for dinner is nearly the same as a hotel room for three people.

A Typical Campground

It's difficult to generalize what the average Latin American campground is like. We've spent nights next to restaurants, on deserted beaches, in RV parks, and in hotel courtyards. Of 55 locations where we paid to camp, slightly more than half were in what we would consider proper campgrounds. That's to say, a park or beach with facilities for campers such as a place to cook, water, bathrooms and showers. If we're lucky there's a covered shelter and a table, but that's not the norm.

The rest of our nights were spent camped next to a hostel, hotel or restaurant that offers camping space along with their normal services. These sites are usually either awesome, or awful. The best places are at hostels that have a kitchen, common room, restaurant, wifi, hot showers and easy access to power outlets. You get all the services and only pay $5 per person to spend the night.

FOR MORE INFO SEARCH LIFEREMOTELY.COM

Five Necessities to Survive Camping

On the other hand, the worst places are often neglected, poorly functioning and dirty due to the fact they are rarely used or the owners simply don't care. It can also be a struggle to fall asleep if you're camped near a noisy common area or restaurant.

Camping Options

In Mexico most campgrounds cater to RVers, specifically expats and snowbirds who drive down every year for the winter. This is OK if you sleep in your vehicle, but it's not ideal for tent campers like us. At least you're almost always guaranteed to find an electrical hookup to charge your electronics.

With the exception of a handful of places in Guatemala and Belize, there are no RV parks in Central America. That's not to say you can't find perfectly reasonable places to park and plug in, they just aren't advertised as such because there are hardly any RVs in Central America.

The best campsites in Central America are in parks and at hostels that offer camping facilities. Amenities range from non-existent to the works. Outside of Costa Rica and parts of Panama the park system is not well developed. Camping is often allowed, and you may have access to a shelter, water, and bathrooms, but the availability of amenities is very inconsistent. Bathrooms and showers tend to be very sub-standard coming from a first-world country. If you have a problem with dirty bathrooms, you should probably spend most of your time in a hotel.

If you are used to car camping in the US or Canada, you'll often find the facilities less than ideal. Plus you rarely have an idea of what's available until you show up. But you get used to it. The more self-sufficient you are, the easier time you'll have of it. At a bare minimum always pack enough drinking water for a day or two, bring the means to purify more, and don't forget a spare roll of toilet paper.

Finding Campsites

FOR MORE INFO SEARCH LIFEREMOTELY.COM

Choosing Campgrounds and Campsites

In the US the best places to camp are state parks and national forests. They are typically much cheaper than national parks, and tend to offer reliable facilities. Private RV parks are another option, although more expensive. RV parks tend to have more facilities such as laundry, wifi, and free hot showers. Searching online is your best bet for finding campsites. Using Google Maps to search in a specific geographic area is also very useful.

Mexico

Finding legitimate campsites in Mexico is also quite easy. The Churchs' book, Traveler's Guide to Mexican Camping, contains a listing of campgrounds throughout Baja and mainland Mexico. We found it to be accurate, although the book tends to cater to RVers, which isn't always optimal for tent campers like us.

Central America

Finding established campgrounds in Central America is a bigger challenge. Camping is not a popular pastime in any country except Costa Rica. Our typical routine for finding camping involves perusing the Lonely Planet guide and spending a good deal of time searching online. Most guidebooks we've found do not list camping options. Lonely Planet is sometimes helpful, but only if you have the individual country books and not the condensed Central America book.

The vast majority of our Central American campsites have been at hostels or restaurants. In Costa Rica and parts of Panama the park system is well developed and frequently allows tent camping. The major downside is having to a pay the one-time park entrance fee on top of what it costs to camp. It's rarely worth it unless you're planning to spend more than one night. We also found a couple awesome free campsites by talking to other travelers.

We keep maps and lists of the accommodations we've used on our website.

Our campsite at Playa Josecito, Costa Rica, recently featured on the BBC.

Tips for Tent Campers

- Buy a good three-season tent. Don't skimp on the price. Make sure it is superbly waterproof, has mesh all around, and that the design allows for good ventilation and airflow. It can be both very hot and very rainy in Central America.
- Bring extra supplies for tent repair, cleaning, waterproofing and seam sealing. Tents under constant use will wear out, grow mold, and start leaking. You won't be able to buy a respectable replacement in a store.
- Foam sleeping mats are infinitely more durable and less hassle than inflatable mats.
- A cut up yoga mat is a great doormat. It helps to keep from tracking too much sand and dirt into your tent.
- Bring a good sleeping bag and liner. Don't underestimate how cold it can be in Mexico and Central America. It may be sweltering on the beach, but up in the mountains temperatures drop considerably.

20

What We Did Well

After eight months on the road, we've learned a more than a couple lessons. Had it not been for our first major overlanding trip in Africa, we would have learned even more. Both adventures have taught us how we prefer to travel, what we can put up with, and how organized or disorganized we can stand to be.

It should go without saying, but the advice we give in this book, and on our website, stems from our personal choices and experiences. Yours will undoubtedly be different. It may have simply been common sense that worked out well in the end, or more likely we learned a lesson the hard way, by screwing up first.

Pack Well & Test Your Gear

Have a place for everything and keep everything in its place. You'll either figure this out before you leave or, more painfully, while you're on the road. Spend money on durable storage containers. They are worth their weight in gold. Go on trial runs to test your gear. If something isn't useful, leave it at home or accept the fact you'll probably end up giving it away a month or two into your trip.

Research Ahead, Just Enough

The amount of research you do is a personal preference. Many people prefer to stop when they get sick of driving and rely entirely on people they meet on the road for advice on places to go. There's no harm to this approach, but it's not something we choose to do, mostly because of our work commitments. We have to know with some certainty where we're going to be next week. We don't go so far as to plan out activities or make hotel reservations, but we know what's there and have an idea of a couple places to stay.

We also like to have a rough plan of where we want go in a country. We never stick to that plan completely, but it gives us something to look forward to and makes decision making easier when the time comes. Being somewhat informed of what lies ahead also helps when we're comparing notes with other travelers or asking advice from a local.

Meet Up With Other Overlanders

There is a huge community of people who have done or are doing overlanding trips in Latin America. South Americans heading north, and North Americans heading south. You will invariably meet up with others going the same way. Hanging out and swapping stories is one of the best parts of this trip. Not to mention getting advice on where to go and helping each other out in tough situations. It's hugely beneficial, and fun.

Check out the Roadtripper Profiles page on Drive the Americas and the In Progress Adventures and Completed Adventures forums on Expedition Portal for lists of past, present and future overlanders.

Home on the Highway, Drive Nacho Drive and Life Remotely camped at Selva Madre trout farm in Costa Rica.

Drive Less

Our Africa trip covered over 12,000 miles in three months. It was hell. On this trip we hit the 10,000-mile mark after seven months on the road. Combining stressful driving conditions with long days on the road is exhausting and rarely leaves you with enough energy to see the sights.

Plenty of people do this trip with a shorter time frame than us. It is possible; just know what you're getting yourself into. We try to avoid driving more than five or six hours in one day. We also try to space out back-to-back long days with a rest day.

Bring a Car That's Easy to Repair

We've been in the shop a couple times for very minor repairs, something just about any mechanic with the proper tools could have fixed. While this bit of advice has yet to truly pay off for us, we have friends with similar vehicles (Toyota 4Runner) that have been repaired plenty of times without much hassle. Finding a decent mechanic is tricky, but at least you know it's possible to find replacement parts when you need them.

We've heard more than one horrific story of overlander breakdowns on the road. Unless the thought being stranded in a foreign country for a month while replacement parts are shipped to you by boat sounds appealing, drive something that can be repaired everywhere!

Vary Your Accommodations

It doesn't matter how much you like to camp, or how great that cushy room with AC feels, mixing up where you spend your nights is a good idea. You'll also miss out on a lot of cool, random happenings if you spend all of your time in one type of place. Hostels are great for meeting other travelers, and camping is the best (and cheapest) way to enjoy nature. Budget hotels are a good place to meet people from the area, and cushy hotels are helpful if you need to spend some time relaxing and getting cleaned up.

Stop For a Bit

Roughly every two months we like to stop and stay in the same place for a week or so. It gives us a chance to relax after long stretches on the road. It's also a great time to clean out our car, repair gear, wash our camping equipment, and catch up with the rest of the world. We're always happy to get back on the road again, but it's crucial for our sanity to periodically stop, rest, and re-evaluate.

Invite Friends and Family to Visit

We've had visitors on three occasions during our trip. In Cabo San Lucas, Antigua, and Costa Rica. It takes a quite a bit of time to sort out the logistics, but for us it's been worth it. Each time we arranged a place where we could all stay together for a week to ten days. If we wanted to drive around, we took short day trips and either rented a car or figured out public transportation.

On a more selfish note, this is a great way to get parts of your trip funded. If you can arrange, chauffeur, guide, and cater a vacation for your folks it's certainly going to cost them less than any other option. It's also a great way to resupply on stuff you've run out of, forgot, or need to replace. And it gives you a way to send souvenirs back home for cheap.

PART 3:

COUNTRIES

21

USA

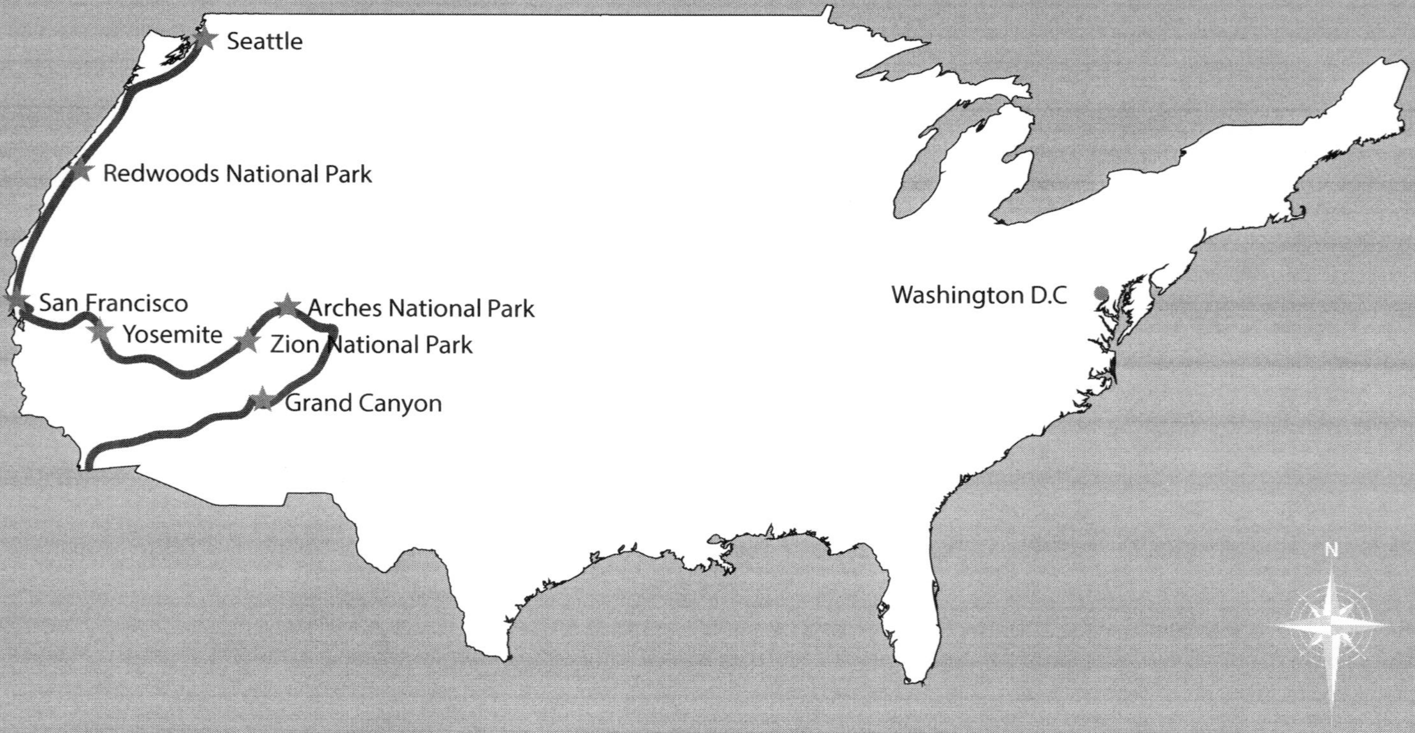
Seattle
Redwoods National Park
San Francisco
Yosemite
Arches National Park
Zion National Park
Grand Canyon
Washington D.C
N

Quick Facts

Currency

US dollars

Cost of premium gas

$3.93/gallon

Our per diem for 3 people

$126.93

Best local drink

Stone Brewery's Arrogant Bastard Ale

Best street food

In-N-Out Burger

Best places to visit

Seattle, Yosemite, Zion, Death Valley

Budget & Money

Currency:	US dollars
Exchange rate:	1 US dollar = 16,000 Vietnamese dong
Are dollars accepted?	Of course
Cost of premium gas:	$3.93/gallon
Miles driven:	3,720
Our per diem for 3 people:	$126.93

Per Diem Breakdown

Lodging	$839.00	24%
Gas	$744.73	21%
Eating Out	$653.00	19%
Groceries	$488.00	14%
Coffee/Booze	$259.00	7%
Firewood, Charcoal & Fuel	$143.00	4%
Gear	$133.00	4%
Park Fees	$110.00	3%
Vehicle Maintenance	$54.00	2%
Tolls & Parking	$21.00	1%
Entertainment	$21.00	1%
Laundry	$19.00	1%
Internet	$17.00	1%
Transportation	$12.00	1%

Food & Accommodation Breakdown

Percent Time Camping	92%
Average Camping Cost	$27.58
Average Hotel Cost	$88.50
Daily Food Expenses	$40.75

Tips

- Eating dinners out is expensive. For the cost of three dinners we could have bought two weeks worth of groceries for three people.
- Expect to pay more for camping if you want showers, laundry and wifi. It may cost $20 to stay in a state park, but an RV park with tent camping and all of the amenities will be more like $30 or $35 near popular destinations.
- Free wifi in internet cafés is not free. If you sit in a coffee shop, you should buy something to drink or have breakfast or lunch. Those costs can add up.
- Free wifi at a campsite is a big bonus. The weather can be a hassle, if it rains you may need to hole up in the laundromat, or if it's sunny, find shade. Either way, if you need to spend a day online, wifi camping is probably your cheapest option.
- Long driving days tend to be the most expensive on average. One or two fill-ups at the gas station and the possibility of eating out for lunch or dinner will easily run you over budget. Pack lunches and plan easy-to-cook dinners once you arrive at your location.

Our Favorite Places

Seattle

We live here, so of course it's one of our favorite places. If you can tolerate incessant gray skies and drizzly days, you too may enjoy this fine city. The weather in August and September cannot be beat. Pike Place Market is the best place for fresh produce and seafood downtown, but don't expect it to be cheap. Chinatown in the International District has great restaurants and plenty of cheap Asian markets. Great places to stay and camp within an hour north, south and west of the city. Look for state parks, camping will be cheaper than national parks and private RV parks.

Zion National Park

A huge national park in Utah, excellent hikes, facilities and camping. The narrows canyon hike is unbelievable, but check conditions at the ranger station. We visited in October, the water wasn't too high, but it was freezing cold. Still worth the effort. You can camp in the park, but you may need reservations. There are plenty of RV parks in the area as well, prices are steeper but facilities are better.

Yosemite National Park

The mother of all national parks in California. Don't miss it. This park is high in the Sierras so if you're there in winter road conditions change frequently. Camping in the park is well worth it but likely requires reservations in advance. There is an easy online booking system.

Death Valley

The lowest point in North America, it is hot. Try 104 in winter. Jared complained the entire time, but it was still a beautiful place to visit. Camping is cheap, but sweltering. It's good practice if you're headed to Nicaragua. Watch out for scorpions, bring a cooler of beer and don't forget a star chart.

Driving & Roads

GPS & Paper Maps

If you need a paper map you can pick up a Rand McNally in most gas stations and supermarkets.

Open Street Maps has pretty good coverage of the US. You can buy US maps through Garmin for about $100. We had an old Nuvi GPS with maps that we used until we hit the Mexico border, then we sent it back home.

Road Conditions

Compared to the rest of your trip, roads will be in excellent condition. National and state parks roads can be dirt or gravel but are usually very well maintained. Forest service roads will be dirt and can be rough, depending on the season.

There are more traffic cops in the US than anywhere else. Watch your speed, especially in school zones.

Internet & Wifi

General availability: Very high
Quality of bandwidth: Excellent if signal strength is high
Frequency of internet in hotels: Very high
Frequency of internet in campgrounds: Very high in RV parks, medium in other campsites, low in national parks.
Average cost to connect: Usually free. Places with fee usually charge $1/hour or $5/day, but costs can run as high as $10/hour.

The Bottom Line

Compared to the rest of the world, finding free wifi in the USA is easy. However, it does help to know where to look.

Coffee Shops, Cafés, and of Course, Starbucks

Where there are coffee and chairs, there is wifi. During our four weeks on the road we did not find a coffee house that didn't have internet access. Combination café/internet cafés are the best. They expect you to whip out your laptop and sit there all day.

Don't Be a Leech

It is debatable if these places are actually free. Since we're addicted to coffee anyway, we consider it two great things for the price of one.

Always remember good internet café etiquette. If the wifi is free, a drink every two hours is polite. If there is a charge, don't feel compelled to order anything, but use your judgment. Most places offer free wifi with a purchase. But sticking around all day, skipping lunch and ordering one short cappuccino isn't good karma.

You Can Always Count on Starbucks and McDonald's

We know they are an evil chain putting quaint hometown coffee shops out of business since 1971, but if your GPS says there is a Starbucks in town, you know for sure there is free wifi. McDonald's tried out free wifi in Australia and recently brought it to the US. Throughout the recession, more and more chains have added free wifi in hope of attracting customers: Barnes & Noble, Panera Bread, Buffalo Wild Wings, Whole Foods Market and Walmart all offer free internet.

Your Local Library

Almost every public library in the US offers free internet access. Most are starting to add wifi as well. If you need to use a computer terminal, it is likely you will have to make a reservation and your time will be limited. Assuming you have your own laptop, connecting to the wifi and finding a nice quiet place to sit will be easy. Just don't go making Skype calls, that'll get you an angry "SSSHHHHHhhhhh" from the librarian.

The Middle of Nowhere

Like a lot of travelers, we are drawn to out-of-the-way places. Often these attractions don't draw enough attention to warrant the variety of lodging options as more popular destinations. You're lucky if there is one overpriced "luxury" lodge and a dust-hole of a campground.

We've discovered that the luxury lodges almost always have internet, but never a room we could afford. The solution: stay in a cheap campground and visit the lodge's café, restaurant, or lobby for a few hours. Most places will require a password, and occasionally a small fee. Politely asking the receptionist or barista will usually get you the info you need, regardless of where you are staying.

Sleep Where There's Wifi

It has become practically mandatory for RV parks, hostels, motels, hotels and resorts to offer internet access. Thankfully this service is free at most touristy places in the US. In business hotels, cities, or remote areas, this might not be the case. It is safe to say that our experience in the western US has been much more positive than, for example, the Australian outback.

Guidebooks Are Always Out of Date

When it comes to internet availability we've often found that the guidebook is wrong. Internet and cell phone networks are expanding faster than new editions can be printed. It is highly likely that your campground or motel will have added wifi access even if the guidebook doesn't list it. A quick phone call or look at their website will confirm.

Desperation

Let's face it, sometimes you're in the middle of a 10-hour drive and you just need to download one stupid file so you can finish a project. Who wants to search for a café, stop and order an espresso, or figure out whether that access code contains capital letters?

Find the main road in the town, drive down it as slow as possible, and constantly hit the refresh button on your wifi search box. You will find an open network, and it won't take long. Connect, download, and get on with your day.

USB Modems & Cell Phones

Costs

Prepaid modem: $30-$180
Prepaid SIM card: $5 (T-Mobile) $2 (AT&T, ordered from Amazon.com)
Cost per minute within the USA: Between $.10 and $.33 for prepaid depending on the amount of minutes you buy at once.

Providers

- AT&T
- T-Mobile
- Verizon Wireless: Note that Verizon Wireless runs on the CDMA network and does not sell or support the use of GSM (SIM cards). We don't recommend you buy a phone or sign up for a plan with Verizon unless you already have the hardware and don't mind ditching it once you cross into Mexico. Every country south of the border uses GSM.

Frequencies

- Voice: GSM-850 and GSM-1900
- Data: Usually 3G 850 and 3G 1900, some companies use 3G 1700 or 3G 2100

USB Modems

USB modems are uncommon in the US, most people have high speed internet in their homes and on their smart phones.

If you have an unlocked USB modem you can pick up a SIM card from an AT&T store and sign up for a prepaid data package. More info on the packages can be found on the AT&T website.

If you need to buy the hardware, T-Mobile offers the best Prepaid USB modem options for around $50.

We ordered an unlocked 3G modem before we left home, it cost about $30 from Amazon.com.

Prepaid Phones

All phone carriers offer some type of prepaid phone plan. If you have an unlocked GSM phone you can pick up a SIM card at AT&T or T-Mobile and sign up for a prepaid in the store or online.

The prepaid rates for calling and data are better with T-Mobile. At one time their coverage was questionable, but it has improved in recent years.

Related Articles

For more detailed information search LifeRemotely.com for the following related articles:

USA Wifi Report: It's all good news

USA Budget Recap

One Gigantic Hole in the Ground

Canyonlands National Park

Arches National Park

Up a Creek Without a Paddle

Confessions of a Desert Rat

It's a Dry Heat

Yosemite

San Francisco

Redwoods

Let's Get this Show on the Road

22

Mexico

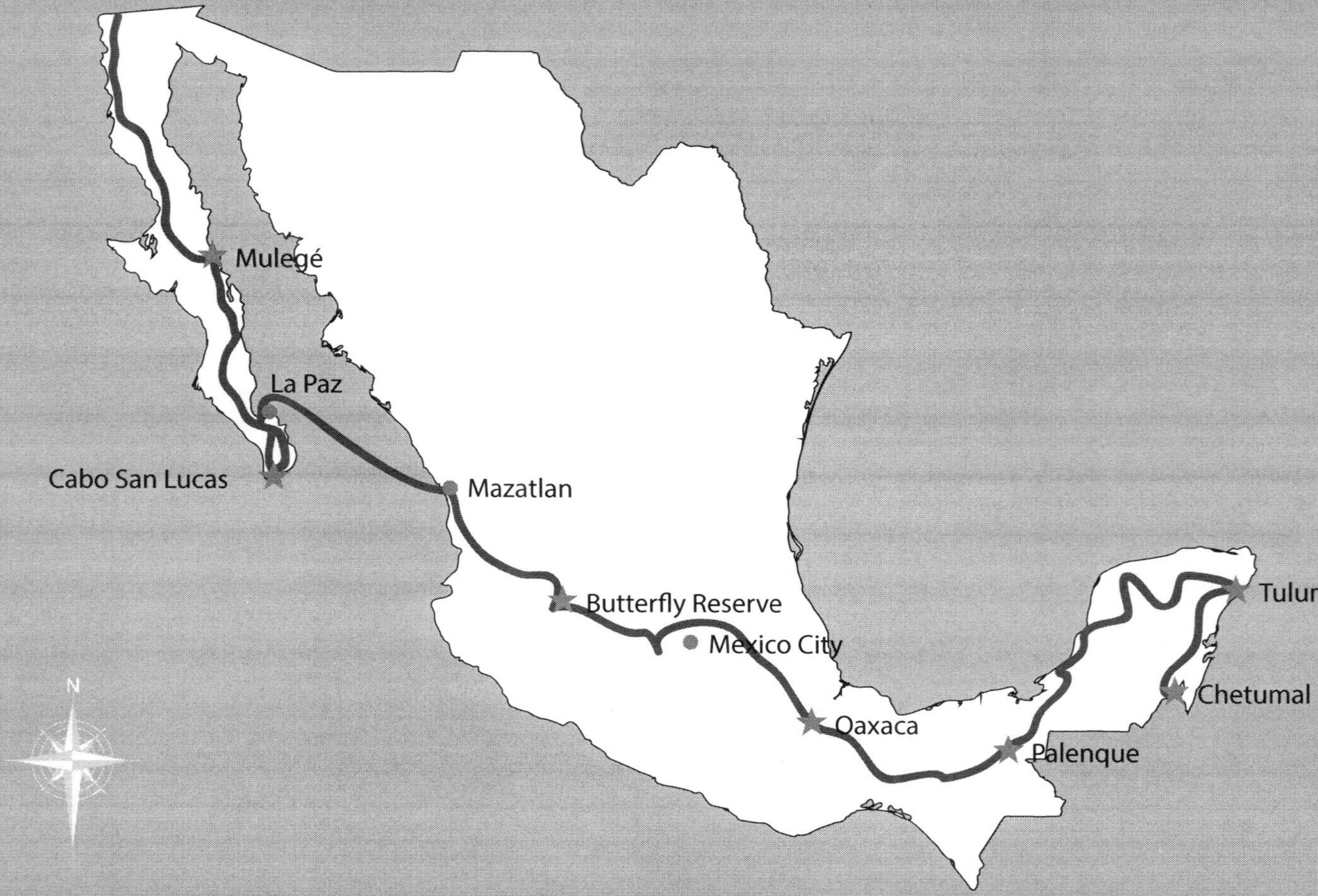
Mulegé
La Paz
Cabo San Lucas
Mazatlan
Butterfly Reserve
Mexico City
Oaxaca
Palenque
Chetumal
Tulum
N

Quick Facts

Currency

Pesos

Exchange rate

13 pesos = 1 US dollar

Cost of premium gas

$2.98/gallon

Our per diem for 3 people

$72.26/day

Best local drink

Mescal

Best street food

Tacos al pastor

Best places to visit

Baja beaches, Mayan ruins, monarch butterfly sanctuary

Budget & Money

Currency:	Pesos
Exchange rate:	13 pesos = 1 US dollar
Are dollars accepted?	In tourist areas
Cost of premium gas:	$2.98 / gallon
Miles driven:	4454
Our per diem for 3 people:	$72.26 for 70 days

Per Diem Breakdown

Lodging	$1,209.92	23.33%
Groceries	$1,155.25	22.27%
Eating Out	$936.76	18.06%
Gas	$743.86	14.34%
Coffee/Booze	$336.58	6.49%
Transportation	$335.33	6.47%
Tolls/Parking	$176.47	3.40%
Park Fees	$161.98	3.12%
Phone/Internet	$133.44	2.57%
Firewood, Charcoal & Fuel	$59.18	1.14%
Border Crossing	$55.75	1.07%
Entertainment	$54.98	1.06%
Supplies	$42.94	0.83%
Laundry	$37.64	0.73%
Gifts	$30.62	0.58%
Vehicle Maintenance	$0	0%

Food & Accommodation Breakdown

Percent Time Camping	73%
Average Camping Cost	$17.10
Average Hotel Cost	$31.21
Daily Food Expenses	$29.70

One-Time Expenses

Vehicle import fee: $55
Baja to Mazatlan ferry: $335

Tips

- Perhaps our biggest surprise was the huge variety of prices for camping. In the US you almost always pay by the site, in Mexico it can be per person, per tent, per site, per vehicle or whatever the guy that comes around to collect at night says it is. Prices varied from free to almost $40 a night. Typically, beach sites were cheapest but with the fewest amenities (no water/showers) and big RV sites, especially those run by expats, the most expensive.

- Watch out for imported food in grocery stores. A lot of American classics can be twice as expensive - kettle-cooked potato chips, BBQ sauce and baked beans for example.

- If you want to save money and can't camp, find a hotel or hostel with a kitchen. It costs as much to eat dinner out as it does to spend the night in a cheap hotel.

- The cheapest eats are always in the places that look the sketchiest, but that's also some of the best food. Markets with eateries and street vendors sell good cheap food, much less expensive than a sit-down restaurant. If the menu lists prices in US dollars, run away.
- Mexican toll roads are expensive. By law there has to be a free alternative, so you never have to pay tolls if you don't want to. But if you need to get somewhere fast, the toll road is your only option. Free roads go through small towns, and that means tons of speed bumps and much much slower going. We spent $150 on tolls, but we can safely say that saved us at least two days of traveling, frayed nerves and unnecessary car repairs down the road.
- Internet cafés are usually cheap, less than $1 per hour. We also spent a bit of money on prepaid plans for our phone and 3G modem, both of which came in handy quite often.

Our Favorite Places

The Beaches of Baja

Baja is a 1000-mile-long peninsula with incredible beaches, lots of camping, and more gringos than you can imagine. It's an easy way to break into Latin American culture. There isn't much to see in the northern state, but the further south you go, the better the beaches get.

Playa Santaspec near Mulege, Playa Tecolote near La Paz, and all the beaches around Los Barriles are amazing places to pitch a tent, soak up some rays and catch some fish. Expect minimal facilities and you won't be disappointed.

Monarch Buttery Sanctuary

Nestled in the hills west of Mexico City, the butterfly sanctuary is a worthy detour. There are two places to enter the park. We went to both in search of camping, every place was closed so we ended up in a hotel. The hike to the butterflies is relatively short and painless, but it's best done on a sunny day. It was cloudy when we arrived and the butterflies weren't very active.

Oaxaca and Puebla

We didn't think we'd spend much time in the bigger cities of Mexico, but these two proved worth a visit. In Puebla we celebrated the Día de Nuestra Señora de Guadalupe and enjoyed walking around the colonial city, touring museums and chowing down on incredible tacos al pastor. Driving in the city isn't as bad as people make it out to be, there are plenty of secure and inexpensive parking garages.

Oaxaca is a foodie paradise. There is plenty to do and eat in the area, plan to spend a few days and definitely take a cooking course. The food we learned to cook here we've eaten time and again throughout Central America. It helps to know what you can do with local ingredients!

Yucatan

Many overlanders skip over the peninsula. If you are remotely interested in Mayan ruins, take the time to see a few of the big ones here. Palenque and Uxmal top our list. Chichen Itza is packed with hawkers and tourists. Tulum is beautiful because of the ocean scenery, but go early or it will be mobbed. With a little time you can find a cheap places to camp south of Playa del Carmen away from the resorts and drunken tourists.

Driving & Roads

GPS & Paper Maps

Guia Roji is the best paper map you can have for driving in Mexico. Buy it when you cross the border at any medium-sized Pemex station. It should cost around 200 pesos. It's the equivalent of Rand McNally in the US.

Open Street Maps are the best GPS maps, but still nothing compared to the Guia Roji book.

Road Conditions

Road conditions in Mexico are worse than the US but not nearly as bad as advertised. Main highways and toll roads are up to US standards. Secondary roads between smaller towns are usually paved and well maintained. Speed bumps (topes) are everywhere. Often placed in seemingly useless places, they ruin an otherwise painless day of driving. Get used to them, they don't go away once you leave Mexico.

Tolls Roads

To take the toll road, or not to take the toll road: that is the question. Thankfully, for a road in Mexico to charge a toll there must be an alternate route. Meaning it is possible to travel the entire country without paying a fee. Unfortunately, the law doesn't specify how well maintained non-toll roads need to be. Most go through many small towns and all are riddled with speed bumps. The extra time, gas and wear on your vehicle may not be worth the savings.

We drove over 4500 miles in Mexico and took toll roads whenever we could. Our total cost was $150. Most of that money was spent between Mazatlan and Oaxaca via Guadalajara and Puebla.

Driving in Mexico City

There are several driving restrictions in Mexico City and the surrounding state. At least one day of the week you are not permitted to drive depending on your license plate. The day we planned to visit Mexico City was a blackout day for all foreign vehicles. The fines were steep and the hassle of driving in the city was big enough that we decided to circumvent it altogether. Look into the rules before you enter the city, they change frequently.

Police & Military Checkpoints

There are occasional police and military checkpoints as you drive through Mexico. Be polite and courteous and you won't have any hassles. Most officers are only looking for guns and drugs. Expect military checkpoints between states, especially around Chiapas and close to the US border.

Local and state police are more notorious for asking for bribes. A persistent, but polite way of denying the request for money (like saying "no entiendo" repeatedly), usually gets them to give up. We had no troubles at any checkpoints, were never treated unfairly and no bribes were attempted.

At military checkpoints between states you may be asked to leave your car. On two occasions we were pulled to the side while officers inspected the inside of our vehicle. You do have a right to ask them to inspect one door at a time which makes it easier to keep an eye on wandering hands. Both times we were stopped it was very clear the officers were only looking for guns and drugs. At one location they brought out a German shepherd to sniff the inside of our car. In both cases we were back on the road within fifteen minutes.

Baja Ferry to the Mainland

A vehicle ferry operates between La Paz on the peninsula and either Mazatlan or Topolombopo on the mainland. Mazatlan is a longer ferry ride and slightly more expensive, but the cost in gas to drive south from Topolombopo balances the extra fees. We traveled with Baja Ferries. For our 4Runner it cost about 2000 pesos, which included the driver's ticket. It cost an additional 975 pesos per passenger, plus we paid 500 pesos for a cabin.

You can buy tickets at the Baja Ferries office in downtown La Paz. The process is relatively simple as long as you dealt with the temporary vehicle import permit process when you crossed the border. If you haven't been issued a vehicle permit yet, you will need to go to the banjercito office in La Paz and get one first.

Border Crossing

Paperwork Needed

- Passports
- Car title
- 1 copy of the driver's passport, license, vehicle title and the tourist card issued at immigration
- Credit card for the refundable vehicle deposit

Costs

For visas: $20 USD per tourist card
For vehicles: $48 plus a $200 USD refundable deposit

Visiting Baja California Only

If you are only planning to visit Baja, you do not need to get a vehicle permit. Most people crossing this border never stop at immigration or the banjercito office. If you are planning to take the ferry to Mazatlan you can go to the banjercito in La Paz instead of in Tiujana.

Crossing Into Mexico from the USA

Border name: San Ysidro
Between cities: Chula Vista, USA and Tijuana, Mexico
Total time: 1 hour 15 minutes
Date we crossed: November 4, 2011

Step by Step

1. Drive through the border. It's easy, it's a freeway.

2. Clear Mexican customs. Stop at the gate and push the button. Green light means go, red light means you get waved over to a little side area to be searched. We got a red light, and we were flagged over to the side. The official there spoke about two words of English. "Pets?" No, sir. "Guns?" Noooo, sir. Then he waved us on.

3. Find the banjercito/migración office.
   Our best advice is to stay to the right.
   There are several signs that say various things like "temporary vehicle permits" or "tourist vehicle imports". None, oddly enough, mention the words we knew like "migración" and "banjercito." If you follow the signs for about a half mile and drive in the general direction of the giant golden arches, you will find the banjercito office.

   GPS coordinates are: Latitude: 32°32'24.19"N Longitude: 117° 1'54.76"W. There is secure parking behind the building.

4. Go to the migración office and fill out the tourist card paper.

5. Go to the banco and pay the tourist card fee. The bank and banjercito are the same place at this crossing. The official will take your tourist card and money and issue receipts.

6. Go back to the migración office with your receipt and get a stamp on your tourist card.

7. Go to the copy shop and make copies of your vehicle permit and the vehicle owner's passport, tourist card and green card (if applicable).

8. Go back to the banjercito line. Give the official copies and originals of your vehicle title and the driver's ID. Pay the vehicle import fee. Give him a credit card for the vehicle deposit. Our credit card was

charged $200 for the deposit, plus another $48 for the permit. He gave us a receipt back, as well as a letter and a sticker for the windshield.

All payments were actually withdrawn in pesos at the current exchange rate. The $200 was refunded when we crossed the border into Belize, but we had to stop at the banjercito there and return the permit.

9. Affix the registration sticker to your car. An official will likely check it when you leave the secure parking lot.
10. Have a taco.
11. Get outta Tijuana.

Internet & Wifi

General availability: Very high
Quality of bandwidth: Like a box of chocolates, you never know what you're going to get. Quality and reliability are higher in internet cafés than in hotels.
Frequency of internet in hotels: Medium most places. High in touristy areas.
Frequency of internet in campgrounds: Zero in campgrounds. Medium in RV parks. High if there is a hotel associated with the camping/RV area.
Average cost to connect: Usually free. Places with a fee usually charge $10-20 pesos ($.75-1.50) per hour

The Bottom Line

Internet in Mexico is plentiful, but not reliable. If you need a steady connection, invest in a TelCel 3G modem (USB dongle). A powerful external wireless card with an antenna is also a good purchase, especially if you plan to stay in a lot of campgrounds. If you are going to setup a phone for making calls it doesn't cost much extra to add a data plan. Be sure to take your passport when you head to the phone store.

Connections

Although internet is easy to find, the quality of the connection is a mixed bag. In our two months crossing Mexico we had many instances of internet failure.

Bandwidth = 10kbps: The most frequent problem we ran into was a super slow connection. Roughly 25% of the time the internet was painfully slow. 1995 slow. Usually it came and went and with some patience we could eventually get our work done. However, if you have to make a scheduled conference call via VOIP or upload or download large files, you are out of luck.

Could not connect: In about 25% of our hotels or campgrounds, one or all of us could not connect to the network. Or we could connect, but there was no data being sent or received. Most of the time we could convince the owner to reset the router and the connection would pick up. Other times it was obviously necessary to call a technician and that usually meant resorting to a backup plan.

Too many users: In two locations we ran into the issue of too many users on one internet connection. We'd find that two of us could connect, but as soon as the third person logged on, someone else would get kicked off.

Poor signal strength: We discovered that in the US and Mexico wifi signals often wouldn't reach our campsite, or even the quiet corner of the restaurant. In Cabo San Lucas we purchased two USB powered external wireless cards. They work great when trying to pick up signals from a distance, and they also double as an extra wireless card. Occasionally we feared that the connection issues were the fault of our laptop's internal wireless cards. Having a spare removes that variable.

Internet Availability by Location

Hotels & Hostels

Hostels always have some type of internet. Most have managed to install wifi, even if the guidebook says otherwise.

Hotels are a bit of a mix. Cheaper hotels in non-touristy areas will not likely have internet. Hotels that cost more than $700 pesos ($53 USD) a night will probably have internet. Hotels in touristy areas, like Cabo, Oaxaca, Merida, San Cristobal de las Casas and other big resort towns will all have internet.

RV Parks and Campgrounds

Most campgrounds in Mexico are actually RV parks. There's a lot more business to be had from RV'ers coming down from the US and Canada than from hobo tent campers like ourselves. Quite a few RV parks do have wifi. If the campground is part of a restaurant or a hotel it's more likely to have wifi. Although, this is not always true or reliable, more than once the internet was down or no longer available when we arrived.

The Traveler's Guide to Mexican Camping book by Terri and Mike Church is invaluable for determining where to camp and which campgrounds have wifi. Although it's a bit out of date, and a couple of the parks listed are closed, the wifi information is still the best you can find for camping.

Internet Cafés

Everywhere. Seriously. If the town is on the map, there will be an internet café. Be aware cafés in small towns are likely to close for siestas (just like all other shops in town). Tourist areas will have dozens of internet cafés.

Regular Cafés

While there is no shortage of cafés, especially in mainland Mexico, not too many have internet. Bigger towns, like Oaxaca, Guadalajara, Puebla, and Merida will usually advertise internet access at coffee shops. But, unlike the USA, this is not the norm.

USB Modems & Cell Phones

Costs

Prepaid modem: $41 with Telcel
Prepaid SIM card: $12 with Movistar
To call the USA per minute: $.15 (2 pesos)

Providers

- Movistar: Cheap, easy to setup, no coverage in remote areas.
- Telcel: More hassle to setup, more expensive, better coverage.

Frequencies

- Voice: GSM-1900
- Data: 3G 850

USB Modems

In Mexico we setup two types of prepaid data connections via cell phone network. In the US we bought an unlocked 3G Android phone and an unlocked USB 3G modem. The day we crossed into Mexico we bought SIM cards for both devices and setup prepaid accounts. The phone was used both for calling and for checking email. The modem came in handy when we needed to reply to an email in the middle of a long drive or when the internet in our hotel or campsite went down. About half way through our time in Mexico we also purchased a new proprietary USB 3G modem from Telcel.

Prepaid USB dongle plans are amazing. We were skeptical when we started, but this little modem prevented many missed deadlines and angry clients. Easily worth its weight in gold!

When we first entered Baja we bought a SIM card for our unlocked 3G modem from Movistar. We checked with Telcel too, but didn't have the patience to wait at the office for a few hours to get it setup. It cost $200 pesos ($15 USD) for the card from Movistar and it came with 3GB free for the first month.

Our experience with the Movistar dongle wasn't great. It worked fine for the first two weeks, except for the distinct lack of coverage in a few key areas. Then one day it ran out of money. Slightly impossible, knowing that we used less than 500mb total. We didn't have the patience to try and sort out the problem. It could have been related to our modem, or it could have been a problem with the account.

After three weeks in Mexico we bought a second dongle, this time from Telcel. It was a royal pain in the butt, but we eventually found an official Telcel center (not a distributor), and things went smoothly. Telcel doesn't sell SIM cards separately, and given our bad experience with Movistar we thought we'd pay the full price for the modem.

For $540 pesos ($41 USD) we had a shiny new 3G modem with another free 3GB of data, which expired in 30 days. It took a while to get it to work in the store, the Movistar software conflicted with the Telcel software and technical support had to be called in. It wasn't such a big deal, lesson learned: always test the modem in the store!

The Telcel modem was excellent. It worked everywhere, even while driving on freeways in the middle of nowhere. In some places we couldn't get a reliable 3G signal and the connection was painfully slow. Most of the time it would have been difficult to download anything over 100mb or do any type of video or voice calling. We did successfully complete several uploads over 50mb, it took a while, but it worked.

Recharging with Telcel is more expensive than with Movistar. 3GB will cost another $500 pesos ($38 USD). Even though it's a bit more expensive and a hassle to purchase, I'd recommend the Telcel 3G data modem over Movistar simply because the coverage is so much better.

Prepaid Phones

Using a local prepaid SIM card for phone calls was simple. We already had an unlocked quad-band phone. We purchased a Movistar SIM card in Ensenada for $150 pesos ($12). Movistar was our choice because of the ridiculously cheap rate to call the US. Investigate up to date calling rates before you buy!

We used this phone for scheduled conference calls every week. It was also cheap enough that we used it to call home every now and then to let Mom know we're still alive

We recharged the phone several times during the two months we spent in Mexico without a hassle. Be aware that the free minutes that come with recharging are not valid for international calls. Movistar has a buy-one-get-one-free deal when buying time, but it took us a while to figure out that the free minutes only work for calls within Mexico.

If you are going to stay in remote areas, it's probably better to go with Telcel. If you will be calling the US or Canada often, stick with Movistar and save some cash.

Recharging

Recharging (adding money to your prepaid account) is simple. Find a shop with a big "Recarga" sign out front. All supermarkets and Oxxo's will be able to recharge. Give the people at the counter your money and your phone number. They will put the money on your account. You will get a text message within a few minutes confirming your recharge.

Once the money is on the account you have several choices. You can use it for voice calls with no further action required. Or you can send a text to sign up for data packages. The number you text and the message determine what type of package you are signing up for.

Recharging USB modems is similar to phone data plans. The SIM card in the device has a phone number assigned to it, don't lose it, you need it to recharge. Add money to that phone number just like you would with a phone. Once the money is on the account you have to choose which plan you want. You can use the software included with the modem to send an SMS, or you can put the SIM card in a phone and send a text from the phone.

Note that if you are using an unlocked dongle from another country you may not be able to install the software for that company. We were not able to use the Movistar software with the dongle we bought in the US, and had no easy way to check our balance.

Checking Balances

We found it to be a total pain to check the balances on all of our devices. There is probably a simple SMS way to get your balance, but we could never sort it out.

Eventually, after a lot of trial an error we did manage to setup an account for our phone at the MiMovistar website. There we could access our balance, and see a list of all of our calls. We went through the same steps to setup an account for our Movistar data modem, and never got it to work.

With Telcel, we could use the software on our computer to see how much data we used, but it only totaled for the computer it was plugged into. Because we used the dongle on three different machines, finding the balance was a pain.

Related Articles

For more detailed information search LifeRemotely.com for the following related articles:

Mexico Wifi Report: Plentiful, But Not Reliable

Mexico Budget Recap

Chicken Pizza

Ruins, Ruins and S'more Ruins

Prepaid Phone and Internet in Mexico

From Mountains to Jungle

Oaxaca

Central Mexico: A Tale of Butterflies and Earthquakes

Cabo San Lucas to La Paz

This F'ing Road Will Kill Ya!

Mulege to Los Barriles

(Almost) White Sandy Beaches

We're Not in Kansas Anymore

23

Belize

Sarteneja
Caye Caulker
Belize City
Belize Zoo
N

Quick Facts

Currency
Belize dollars

Exchange rate
2 Belize dollars = 1 US dollar (fixed)

Cost of premium gas
$5.46/gallon

Our per diem for 3 people
$95.79

Best local drink
Belikin Stout

Best street food
Budget Man specials on Caye Caulker

Best places to visit
Sarteneja and the Cayes

Budget & Money

Currency:	Belize dollars
Exchange rate:	2 Belize dollars = 1 US dollar (fixed)
Are dollars accepted?	Everywhere
Cost of gas:	$5.46/gallon
Miles driven:	198
Our per diem for 3 people:	$95.79

Per Diem Breakdown

Eating Out	$246.00	27.16%
Transportation	$180.00	19.87%
Lodging	$176.50	19.49%
Groceries	$152.48	16.83%
Coffee and Booze	$58.50	6.46%
Park Fees	$45.00	4.97%
Vehicle Import	$28.00	3.09%
Gas	$25.00	2.76%
Laundry	$10.00	1.10%
Tolls and Parking	$7.88	0.87%
Charcoal and stove fuel	$2.50	0.28%
Misc. Supplies	$2.00	0.22%

Food & Accommodation Breakdown

Percent Time Camping	73%
Average Camping Cost	$14.56
Average Hotel Cost	$20.00
Daily Food Expenses	$32.41

One-Time Expenses

- Border crossing - $28 USD
- Ferry to Caye Caulker from Sarteneja - $180 USD

Tips

- If you go out to the cayes, especially the popular ones, spend some time shopping around for good lodging deals. We found a hotel room for $15 a night for three people, and it wasn't listed anywhere. There was barely a sign on the street. Just ask around, people in Belize are very friendly and everyone speaks English.

- Same goes for eating out. Shop around to find the best deals. It seems like lunches are big meals, so if you're not into eating heavy while the sun's up you can usually get enough to split with two people or save for a second meal later.

- Fill up on gas in Mexico or Guatemala. And leave the country on empty, there are gas stations just over both borders.

- It's a lot cheaper to take a ferry to the northern cayes from Belize City than Sarteneja or Corozal. We didn't want to leave our car in Belize City, and we were already in Sarteneja, but we could have saved $100.

Our Favorite Places

Sarteneja

Nestled out in the northeastern tip of Belize, Sarteneja is a quiet place to spend a few days. The owners of Backpacker's Paradise, a hostel with camping, a restaurant and wifi, are helpful and welcoming. The drive out here takes a bit of patience. Stop in Corozal Town and pick up groceries, there isn't much in Sarteneja.

You do not need to go all the way to Orange Walk and circle back north. There is a road, complete with two hand crank ferries, that will get you to Sarteneja in a fraction of the time. Most of the roads are dirt but are in good condition during the dry season. If you decide to catch the ferry from Sarteneja to the cayes you can leave your car at Backpacker's Paradise for $5 per day.

Caye Caulker

The most laid back of all the cayes, this is the place to be. Shop around for cheap accommodations. We stayed one night at a hostel that cost $35 US, the next day we found a nicer room at a place called Sandy Lane for $15 a night. Everything is more expensive on the island, so be prepared. If you can find a place to cook it's worth it not to have to eat out every meal. You can also camp at several of the hostels if you can pack in the gear. The snorkel tours are highly recommended.

Driving & Roads

GPS & Paper Maps

Best paper map is from Reise Know How.
Open Street Maps and Cenrut.org are the best free GPS maps for Garmin.

Road Conditions

Road conditions in Belize are comparable to Mexico. Speed bumps are common in small towns, but major highways are paved and in decent shape. The roads out to Sarteneja are dirt with a few potholes, but nothing a 2WD couldn't handle.

Police & Military Checkpoints

We encountered fewer police and military checkpoints in Belize, but we did not go to Belize City where crime, and therefore police, are more prevalent.

Border Crossing

Paperwork Needed

- Passports
- Car title

Costs

For visas: Free, but there is a BZ$37.50 exit fee.
For vehicles: $5 USD for fumigation, $23 USD for two weeks of insurance.

Insurance

Buying insurance is mandatory in Belize, but wait to buy it until you have passed through the border area. Touts will constantly try to stop you and tell you the laws have changed. It's a ploy. Wait until you see the giant white insurance building just across the border.

Exit Fee

There are no immigration or vehicle permit fees for entering Belize, but there is an exit fee. Don't ask us how or why it works this way in Belize. When you leave, no matter if by land or by air, you will be required to pay $18.75 USD.

Crossing Into Belize from Mexico

Border name: Santa Elena or simply Chetumal
Between cities: Subteniente López (Chetumal), Mexico and
Santa Elena (Corozal), Belize
Total time: 45 minutes
Date we crossed: January 14, 2012

This border crossing is about 15 minutes outside of the bustling Mexican city of Chetumal, and another 15 minutes from the town of Corozal on the Belizean side. There are smaller towns on the border and a "free zone" if you'd like to stock up on cheap Chinese junk.

Step by Step

1. Go to the Mexican immigration booth, hand in your tourist cards and have your passport stamped. We parked on the right side before the customs roadblock. There is a small dark blue building with a sign in English and Spanish noting that it is the immigration/migración office.

2. Go to the Mexican banjercito and have your vehicle import permit canceled and your vehicle deposit refunded. The banjercito office at this border crossing is on the opposite side of the road, on the left as you approach Belize. It is past the Mexican customs checkpoint. You will need to drive there so the banjercito official can verify your VIN number.

3. Drive over the bridge to Belize. There is a strange "free zone" shopping area, and a lot of touts that try to convince you to buy insurance here. Keep to the road to the right and ignore them. It's maybe a half mile until you see the Belize customs checkpoint.

4. Stop at the fumigation area to have your car sprayed. Because we aren't so good at reading road signs, we drove right past the

fumigation building and the sign out front that says "mandatory stop for all vehicles". Thankfully it wasn't a big deal. However, you should stop here first and pay for the fumigation just to save some time. It's currently BZ$10 dollars for fumigation. You can pay with US dollars or Belizean dollars, but not pesos.

5. Park in the marked lot outside the immigration building.

6. Go to the immigration counter and have your passports stamped or visas issued.

7. Go to the customs counter, present your vehicle title and get an import permit. We were issued a 30-day temporary permit for no charge. They entered information, but did not require any copies of documents. The customs agent asked us to take everything out of the car and bring it through the building for inspection. When we explained we had a lot of crap, and this would take a few hours, she decided that it would be easier for her to inspect the vehicle outside at the customs gate.

8. Go back to the car and drive through the gate, an official may inspect the contents of your vehicle, the VIN and the plates to make sure they match the permit.

9. Stop at the giant, clearly marked insurance building after you clear customs. Three other people offered us insurance during the process of getting through customs. All claimed that we needed to buy before we crossed and all quoted slightly ridiculous prices in US dollars. It's just a ploy. Buy insurance after you cross the border. Total cost was $23 USD for two weeks.

10. Put the insurance sticker on your car windshield.

Internet & Wifi

General availability: Medium to high
Quality of bandwidth: Usually very bad. Few places pay for high speed. Unless you can get a hardline, count on painfully slow connections.
Frequency of internet in hotels: Medium. In tourist areas there's more likely to be internet in a hotel. If you need it, check in advance.
Frequency of internet in campgrounds: Surprisingly high. Most campgrounds were part of a hotel or wildlife sanctuary that also had restaurants with wifi. Every campground we stayed at had internet, but we planned it that way.
Average cost to connect: Free at hotels and campgrounds, BZ$5-$15 ($2.50-$7.50 USD) per hour otherwise. The cayes tend to be higher BZ$15 per hour ($7.50 USD).

The Bottom Line

If you need quality internet all the time, be prepared for inconvenience and extra expense. If you are traveling through Belize for a few weeks, we recommend delaying work until you reach an internet-friendly country, especially if you need to make phone calls or download lots of files.

Internet in accommodations

With a little bit of extra effort you can find any level of accommodation with wifi. Every place we camped had wifi. All hostels seem to have it. Hotels are hit or miss. Cheap hotels don't seem to bother. High-end hotels always have it, but sometimes charge extra.

Bandwidth is usually terrible. Most places we stayed the connection speed was barely dialup quality. BTL charges by the speed, so it makes sense that most places don't bother to pay the extra cost. We did manage to hook up via ethernet cable at one place and were shocked at the how fast it was.

Internet in cafés

The cost of internet in cafés, especially in the cayes, was at least $5 USD per hour and sometimes more. Be aware that many coffee shops and restaurants on the islands have free internet, but they might not advertise it. We walked around San Pedro for an hour looking for a place to have lunch and check emails. Eventually we gave up and went into a random pizza place. It turned out they had free wifi and roasted their own coffee. Lesson learned, just ask.

The BTL problem

BTL's monopoly causes some rather annoying problems for travelers.

Skype is (sort of) blocked. The story here is a bit complicated. Skype.com is certainly blocked. The app (if you already have it installed) will work, but you will need to find internet fast enough to support it. In the past BTL completely blocked Skype in attempt to push their own more expensive VOIP service. It used to be necessary to setup up a private VPN connection to use Skype, but this is no longer the case.

Kindles won't connect. For those of you with a 3G kindle, it won't do you any good in Belize. Shouldn't be a surprise if you've checked out the coverage map. Apparently BTL doesn't have any interest in giving Amazon a piece of their pie. Areas near the Guatemala and Mexico borders, like San Ignacio, are the exception.

Internet is expensive. All internet access here is expensive, so is setting up a cell phone and calling internationally. Compared to Guatemala and Mexico, the costs here are slightly ridiculous. The Belize government also taxes high-speed internet somewhere between 19-24%. It's not surprising that many cheaper hotels don't bother to install it.

USB Modems & Cell Phones

Costs

Prepaid modem: $92.50 USD with Smart
Prepaid SIM card: Unknown
To call the USA per minute: $.26 (with prepaid BTL cards from a pay-phone)

Providers

- Digicell: (owned by BTL) don't be too shocked by their terrible webpage, we swear it is a legitimate company. They have the best coverage and the highest rates. If you want decent information, visit a BTL office. There is one in every major town, although they are always closed on weekends.

- Smart: this company offers better rates but is only CDMA compatible. Our GSM phone wouldn't work on their network. If you have a Verizon phone from the US, they can reprogram it to work with the Smart network for a fee. Reportedly BTL does not let Smart use any of their infrastructure, so the quality and coverage of service is limited.

Frequencies

- Voice: GSM-850 and GSM-1900

USB Modems

We did investigate purchasing a USB dongle through Smart, they quoted us BZ$185 ($92.50 USD) for the dongle, excluding a data package. That was far enough out of our price range that we didn't bother to ask for the data rates.

Digicell advertises that you can buy a SIM card and use it in your phone or modem simply by entering the APN number to connect. They don't have any prepaid data packets; you simply pay $.005 BZ per kilobyte of data. More info is available on the Digicell website.

Prepaid Phones

Smart works similar to Verizon in the US. Their phones don't use SIM cards, so it is expensive to setup a prepaid plan. Unless you happen to have an unlocked CDMA phone, don't bother.

Digicell sells SIM cards and prepaid phone cards. Most towns have a telemedia office where you can arrange everything. Recharge phone cards can also be used at pay phones throughout the country. Because we were only in Belize for a short time, we bought one of the prepaid cards and used the pay phone at our hostel for calling the US.

Related Articles

For more detailed information search LifeRemotely.com for the following related articles:

Belize Campgrounds and Hotels

Belize Budget Recap

Belize Wifi Report: One Giant Monopoly

The Belize Zoo

Hello Central America!

24

Guatemala

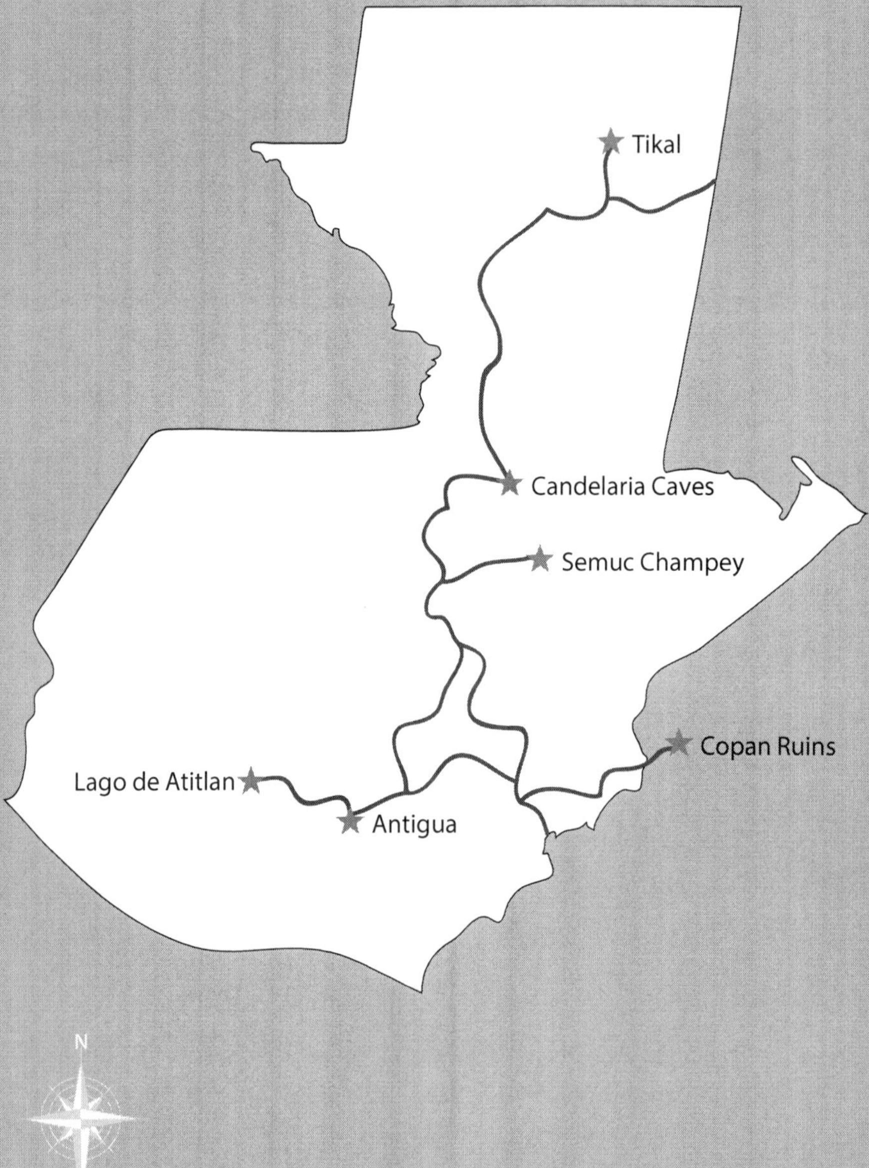
Tikal
Candelaria Caves
Semuc Champey
Copan Ruins
Lago de Atitlan
Antigua
N

Quick Facts

Currency
Quetzal

Exchange rate
8 quetzales = 1 US dollar

Cost of premium gas
$4.92/gallon

Our per diem for 3 people
$106.23

Best local drink
Picocito

Best street food
Tostada mixta

Best places to visit
Candelaria Caves, Tikal, Semuc Champey, Antigua

Budget & Money

Currency:	Quetzal
Exchange rate:	8 quetzales = 1 US dollar
Are dollars accepted?	Rarely
Cost of premium gas:	$4.92/gallon
Miles driven:	1489
Our per diem for 3 people:	$106.23

Per Diem Breakdown

Language School	$1,874.70	29.24%
Home Stay	$1,602.66	25.00%
Eating Out	$591.61	9.23%
Gas	$493.25	7.69%
Groceries	$436.36	6.81%
Lodging	$370.84	5.78%
Vehicle Maintenance	$356.02	5.55%
Supplies	$259.80	4.05%
Transportation	$206.05	3.21%
Park Fees	$140.92	2.20%
Coffee & Booze	$110.88	1.73%
Entertainment	$78.11	1.22%
Phone & Internet	$78.05	1.22%
Laundry	$50.83	0.79%
Tolls & Parking	$25.39	0.40%
Vehicle Import	$23.07	0.36%
Border Fees	$13.35	0.21%

Food & Accommodation Breakdown

Percent Time Camping	39%
Average Camping Cost	$10.01
Average Hotel Cost	$27.34
Total Food Expenses	$1027.97

One-Time Expenses

- Border crossing - $23.76
- Car maintenance, real axle seal replacement - $320

Tips

- If you are going to have big reoccurring expenses (like our homestay and language school) and you care about having enough money for the time you wish to spend, do your homework and figure out exact prices ahead of time.

- If you are signed up for an all-inclusive meal plan, don't forget that you're still going to spend money on food. Drinks, snacks and the occasional meal out will add up.

- If you're driving, consider having an emergency fund for car repairs. We have $1500 budgeted. The $320 we spent on car repairs in Guatemala came out of this fund. We recommend it, not because it matters in terms of the money (it all comes from the same place anyway) but because knowing you have this reserve will help you keep a calm head during potentially stressful times.

- If you are traveling with your car and plan to stay in the same general area for a while, but still want to take a few short side trips, consider taking round-trip public transport instead of driving.

Our Favorite Places

Candelaria Caves

These ancient Mayan caves are in the north of Guatemala, about half way between Tikal and Coban. There's not much info in guidebooks, but this was our favorite place in all of Central America. On the main road south from Tikal you hit a T-junction, right takes you to Copan and left goes to Raxruha.

There is a French restaurant and small hotel on this road where you can arrange a tour; it's hard to miss. We recommend the four-hour tubing tour. It includes two hours of spelunking followed by two hours of tubing through the caves. Guide included, it cost about 300 quetzales a person and was worth every penny.

Tikal

The granddaddy of all Mayan ruins. If you're going to pay to see one ancient city, let this be it. You can camp at the Jaguar Inn in the park where you'll find cold showers, bathrooms and wifi for a fee. Get up early and go straight out to Temple IV. It will likely be empty. You can hike around for half a day then go back to the campsite for a siesta when it's too hot, and return to the ruins in the late afternoon. This is a huge park with tons to see so take your time.

If you only want to spend one night in the park, plan to arrive in the afternoon. They don't allow entry for the following day until 4pm. Factoring in the hour it takes to drive to the park entrance, the earliest you can pass the gate is 3pm.

Antigua

We lived just outside of Antigua in the suburb of San Miguel Escobar for nearly two months. We had good connections with a volunteer organization in the area so we decided to slow down, invest in a homestay, and learn some Spanish. There are tons of Spanish schools in Antiqua. Do your research in advance. If you are looking for some extra immersion, stay with a family for a week or two. Our homestay cost about $70 per week per person, which included three amazing meals per day.

Antigua itself is a beautiful colonial town, occasionally packed with tourists, but not without a few off-the-map places. If you are in the area for Lent or Semana Santa (Easter) check out the Saturday processions. There is one every weekend and they are incredible. You can ask around the central square for a map and schedule of the events.

Semuc Champey

Located just outside of the town of Lanquin, Semuc Champey is another natural area worth visiting. Made up of beautiful blue limestone pools, it's a great place to go for the day, walk around and go for a swim. It's only 15 kilometers from Lanquin to Semuc, but the road is terrible. You can hitch a ride in town for about 30 quetzales per person if you want to save your vehicle the hardship.

Note that the road from Coban to Lanquin will take about two hours. The first 45 kilometers are nicely paved but windy. The last 10 kilometers are on quite possibly the worst road in the country. If you are arriving from Tikal you may want to overnight at Parque Nacional Victoria in the center of Coban.

Driving & Roads

GPS & Paper Maps

Best paper map is from Reise Know How.
Open Street Maps and Cenrut are the best free GPS maps for Garmin.

Road Conditions

Roads in Guatemala are decidedly worse than Mexico and Belize. Most of the highways around Guatemala City were in the process of being rebuilt into four lane highways. Great news for you, lots of traffic for us. The roads in the north around Tikal and Coban are usually paved, but have loads of unexpected potholes and speed bumps.

The dirt road out to Lanquin and Semuc Champey is possibly the worst in the country. We blew an axle seal the first time we drove to Lanquin. Upon returning six weeks later, we blew the other one.

Antiqua Roads and Parking

Because it is a UNESCO site, the cobblestone roads in Antigua must remain unchanged. They can be repaired, but not paved. Driving through Antiqua will be one of the bumpiest experiences of your trip.

To park on the streets in Antigua you need a parking pass. There are uniformed officers every two or three blocks that will sell you a pass for Q10. After a certain hour at night they are no longer required.

Border Crossing

Paperwork Needed

- Passports
- Car title
- 1 copy of the drivers passport and the vehicle title

Costs

For visas: Q20 ($2.60 USD) per person (unofficially)
For vehicles: Q18 ($2.34 USD) for fumigation,
Q160 ($20.78 USD) for the vehicle import permit
Exit fee: If you are coming from Belize you will have to pay
an $18.75 USD per person exit fee

CA-4 Visas

Be aware that even though Honduras doesn't respect the CA-4, all other countries count your time in Guatemala, El Salvador, Honduras and Nicaragua cumulatively. You have 90 days total. No exceptions. Be prepared for steep fines if you overstay.

Crossing Into Guatemala from Belize

Border name: Melchor de Mencos
Between cities: Benque Viejo Del Carmen, Belize and Melchor de Mencos, Guatemala
Total time: 55 minutes
Date we crossed: January 25, 2012

Step by Step

1. Go to the Belize immigration building.
2. Pay the exit fee at the first counter $37.50 BZ ($18.75 USD)
3. Have your passport stamped at the second counter.
4. At the third counter, cancel the vehicle permit.
5. Proceed to Guatemala.
6. First stop is the huge fumigation area. Your car is sprayed automatically as you drive through. Make sure your windows are up! Pay the man (Q18) upon exit and get a fumigation receipt.
7. Walk to the open-air customs and immigration building.
8. Stand in the entrada line. Get your passport stamped and pay the Q20 per person fee. There is no receipt for this fee, it isn't official. We probably could have argued our way out of it, but everyone else was paying it.
9. To the left of the immigration lines are lines for vehicle importation. Present your vehicle title, driver's passport and copies of both documents. He will give you a printed form with your vehicle information and the amount you have to pay which was Q160 for us, but other reports have varied.
10. Go to the cashier window on the other side of the big building. Present the vehicle paperwork and pay the fee. The cashier will stamp the paperwork and return it to you.
11. Go back to the vehicle import counter and show the official your stamped receipt from the cashier. He will issue you a permit sticker for your windshield and give you a paper permit and the receipt. He will keep the copies of your title and the driver's ID.

12. Return to your car, affix the sticker and then drive towards the bridge.
13. An officer will stop you and ask for your permit paperwork. He may take the paperwork to the side and consult with his gun-toting colleagues. He'll return the paperwork and wave you through.
14. We heard that we would be stopped and asked to pay another fee just across the border. Apparently it's a municipality tax that foreign vehicles must pay upon entering Melchor de Mencos. The border official on the Belize side told us that this should legitimately be Q10, although we've heard of people paying Q40 or more. Luckily we weren't stopped. We didn't even see the guard until we saw her stop the guy behind us.

Internet & Wifi

General availability: High
Quality of bandwidth: It's a crap-shoot. Usually low with wifi and high when connected via cables.
Frequency of internet in hotels: High in hostels and mid-range hotels, low in guesthouses or budget hotels.
Frequency of internet in campgrounds: Campgrounds that were part of other lodges or restaurants all had wifi. National parks did not have any type of internet.
Average cost to connect: Free with accommodation. Q10 per hour was a common rate for internet cafés in Antigua.

The Bottom Line

If you need occasional internet, you can count on hotels and internet cafés in tourist areas. If you have to work on a schedule, and can't tolerate terrible speeds and frequent outages, invest in a prepaid USB modem.

Connections

Same as Belize and Mexico, we found that connections were simply unreliable, especially when internet was a free service included with your accommodation or coffee. Frequently the bandwidth was only fast enough for loading simple webpages.

In both hotels, and when living with our family in Antigua, we experienced long periods of "limited connectivity", meaning the internet was down for all intents and purposes. We never clearly identified if this problem was related to the router, the service provider, the number of users, or our computers. But it happened constantly.

Hotels & Hostels

Most hostels will have internet, although it may be painfully slow.

We spent 6 weeks living with a family just outside Cuidad Vieja. They had broadband internet that worked 90% of the time. 90% doesn't quite cut it when we have to get work done, so we used our 3G USB modem as a backup.

Campgrounds

We only stayed in a few campgrounds in Guatemala. Most were connected to restaurants or lodges and consistently had internet. We camped at national parks in Coban and near the Biotopo del Quetzal. Neither had internet, but both had decent cell phone signal strength for the USB modem.

Internet Cafés

Like the rest of the places we have visited, internet cafés are everywhere and seem to have the most reliable and speedy connections. Your odds of finding a café increase if tourists frequent the area. For example, most bars and cafés in Antiqua offer free wifi.

USB Modems & Cell Phones

Costs

Prepaid modem: 205 quetzales ($27 USD)
Prepaid SIM card: 50 quetzales ($6 USD)
To call the USA per minute: $.26

Providers

- Tigo
- Claro
- Movistar

Frequencies

- Voice: GSM 900, 850 and 1900
- Data: 3G 1900

USB Modems

If you need internet on a schedule, pick up a Tigo USB modem. They cost Q205 ($27) for the hardware, and include 15 days and 8 gigs of free service. Recharging for another month costs between Q145 and Q299, depending on how much data you need.

Our Tigo modem worked everywhere and had 3G connectivity. It was excellent to have as a backup when the hostel/campground/restaurant internet died. In most places it was speedy enough that we could hook up our router and share the connection between three computers.

Prepaid Phones

We purchased a new Tigo SIM card for Q50 when we crossed into Guatemala. After a few helpful conversations with a hostel employee we got the low down on the most cost-effective way to call home. The trick is to take advantage of triple saldo promotions. On those days you will get three times the money you add to your prepaid balance. And unlike Mexico, the promotional balance can be used to call internationally. It's tough to know in advance which days are promotional, your best bet is to ask or look for advertisements. Movistar and Claro also offer triple saldo days, although their details may vary.

With Tigo you can also sign up for the "Gringo" plan. Text the word GRINGO to 800 to enroll. With this promo every Q100 you spend (promotional balances don't count), you receive 50 minutes free to call the US or Canada. It's a free plan, so even if you don't think you will use a full Q100, it's worth signing up.

Currently the rate to call the USA is Q2 per minute ($0.26). But if you recharge with triple saldo you can bring that cost to $0.09/per minute. And if you sign up for the Gringo plan, you can save another few cents.

Related Articles

For more detailed information search LifeRemotely.com
for the following related articles:

Guatemala Campgrounds and Hotels

Guatemala Budget Recap

Guatemala Wifi & Phone Report: Buy a USB Modem and Be Happy

You Mean Quetzals? I Don't Think They Exist.

The Best of Alta Verapaz: Semuc Champey and Candelaria

Adios, Antigua

Coffee Tasting in Antigua

These Boots are Made for Walkin...

The Processions of Antigua

Lago de Atitlán

Jessica and the Chocolate Factory

Sand flies, botlas flies, fleas, mosquitoes, no-see-ums, and other unidentified flying biting bugs

Back to School

Bienvenidos a Guatemala!

25

El Salvador

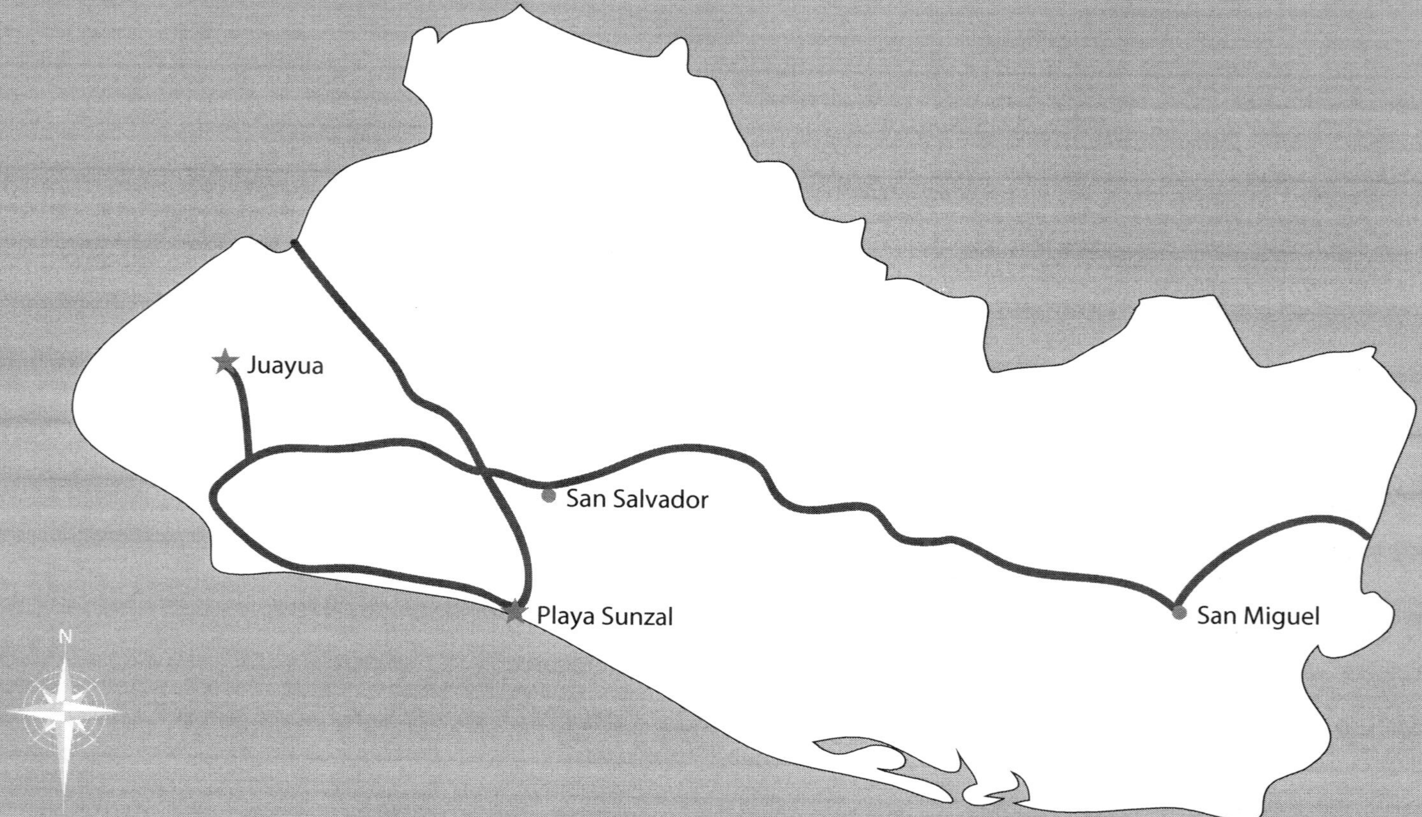
Juayua
San Salvador
Playa Sunzal
San Miguel
N

Quick Facts

Currency
US dollar

Exchange rate
Fixed 1:1

Cost of premium gas
$4.50/gallon

Our per diem for 3 people
$70.30

Best local drink
Coffee

Best street food
Pupusas

Best places to visit
Ruta de Las Flores

Budget & Money

Currency: US dollar

Exchange rate to USD: Fixed 1:1

Are dollars accepted? Obviously

Cost of premium gas: $4.50/gallon

Miles driven: 439

Our per diem for 3 people: $70.30

Per Diem Breakdown

Lodging	$259.00	34.79%
Groceries	$186.75	25.08%
Gas	$99.00	13.30%
Entertainment and Tours	$80.00	10.75%
Eating Out	$69.00	9.27%
Laundry	$16.50	2.22%
Coffee/Booze	$13.75	1.85%
Park Fees	$10.00	1.34%
Camp Fuel, Charcoal, Firewood	$9.00	1.21%
Tolls and Parking	$1.50	0.20%

Food & Accommodation Breakdown

Percent Time Camping	67%
Average Camping Cost	$13.71
Average Hotel Cost	$40.75
Total Food Expenses	$275.00

Tips

- If you care about saving money on food costs, plan ahead and research hotels with kitchens or cooking areas. It's worth paying more for a hotel if you can cook for yourself.
- Spend time researching camping in advance. Guidebooks are practically useless, but with a few hours online or buying beers for other travelers, you can discover cheap and excellent campgrounds.
- Air conditioned rooms are easily 30% more expensive than rooms without, but unless you're accustomed to 95 degree heat, it's worth it for a good night's sleep.
- If you don't want air conditioning make sure you say something if it's unclear what the options are. Hotels may try to sell you the more expensive AC rooms without mentioning cheaper alternatives.

Our Favorite Places

Ruta de Las Flores and Portezuelo Park

The Ruta de las Flores is a beautiful drive through the mountains in central El Sal. There is an incredible place to camp called Portezuelo Park. You can pitch a tent and the grounds keeper will bring you a wheelbarrow full of firewood each night. If you're longing for place in the mountains to cool down and want a good ol' fashion campfire, this is the place.

The food festival happens in Juayua every weekend. It's worth visiting to sample delicious (and very strange) El Salvadorian cuisine.

Driving & Roads

GPS & Paper Maps

Best paper map is from Reise Know How.
Open Street Maps and Cenrut.org are the best free GPS maps for Garmin.

Road Conditions

It's a small country. The roads aren't great, but you never have to drive very far to get where you want to be. The main highways around San Salvador, and the road leading to the border of Honduras are in decent shape, especially relative to Guatemala.

Border Crossing

Paperwork Needed

- Passports
- Car title
- 1 copy of the drivers passport, car title, and canceled Guatemalan permit
- 2 copies of your El Salvadorian vehicle permit

Costs

For visas: $0
For vehicles: $.60 for copies

CA-4 Visas

Be aware that even though Honduras doesn't respect the CA-4, all other countries count your time in Guatemala, El Salvador, Honduras and Nicaragua cumulatively. You have 90 days total. No exceptions. Be prepared for steep fines if you overstay.

Crossing Into El Salvador from Guatemala

Border name: San Cristobal
Closest major cities: El Progreso, Guatemala and Santa Ana, El Salvador
Total time: 1 hour 55 minutes
Date we crossed: March 25, 2012

Step by Step

1. Stop at the small booth on the right side of the road and tell the nice officials you need to have your vehicle permit canceled. They will instruct you where to park. Unlike most crossings, the right and left sides are NOT entry and exit, they are customs and immigration respectively.

2. The SAT (vehicle permit officials) will remove the sticker from your car and double check the VIN and the paperwork you received when entering.

3. The official will walk you to the customs counter and present your paperwork to the officer.

4. Before your paperwork can be canceled your passport must be stamped. Go across the street to the Guatemalan immigration building and have your passport stamped.

5. Return to the customs area and have your permit canceled. The official will need your original permit, vehicle title and the driver's passport. They will take care of making copies if needed. They will return all of the originals except for the permit. They will give you a copy of the canceled permit.

6. Drive through to the El Salvador crossing, another covered drive-through area with a huge building in the center.

7. Go to the copy shop and make a copy of your canceled Guatemalan permit. Also, make sure you have copies of your title and the driver's passport.

8. Park your car on the far right, not in the lane for immigration.

9. Go to the customs windows (the first set), and ask for a temporary permit. They will need your title, driver's passport, canceled Guatemalan permit, and a copy of each of these.

10. Fill out a long form for your permit, you will need to know all the details for your car: VIN, CCs, type of car, color, cylinders, etc (in Spanish).

11. When you have your permit, go back to the copy stand and make two copies. You will surrender one when you leave the border. The other you will need when you leave the country.

12. Drive into the main immigration lane. Wait in your car until you are first in line.

13. Present your passports. Immigration will look at your passports, but usually won't stamp them because El Salvador honors the CA-4 agreement with neighboring countries.

14. Drive about 100 meters to the road block. Hand over both the original and a copy of your El Salvador permit. The official will keep the copy and return the original.

Internet & Wifi

General availability: Medium-high
Quality of bandwidth: In cities, excellent. Everywhere else, good luck.
Frequency of internet in hotels: Medium. Always in hostels and mid to high-end hotels. Not likely in small guesthouses.
Frequency of internet in campgrounds: Low. Only expect internet if the campground is attached to a restaurant or a hotel.

The Bottom Line

Depending on your budget, buy a USB modem or a research your accommodation in advance. Free wifi can be found, but reliable free wifi is rare. If clients are waiting, don't mess around, get a 3G modem.

Connections

The story here is the same as the rest of Central America. Internet is available in cafés in pretty much every town, always in hostels, usually in hotels and rarely in campgrounds. But, connection speeds and reliability varies dramatically.

We stayed at a hostel in San Salvador with amazing wifi for three days. But we also stayed at a hotel in Santa Ana, and another in San Miguel, where at least one of us couldn't connect, or was constantly kicked off the network.

Camping areas that are connected to hostels or restaurants offer the best chance of wifi access. If you have appointments to keep, invest in a USB modem, or go to a café to connect.

USB Modems & Cell Phones

Costs

Prepaid modem: $18 USD
Prepaid SIM card: $3
To call the USA: $.75 for 30 minutes

Providers

- Claro
- Digicel
- Tigo

Frequencies

- Voice: GSM-850, GSM-900, GSM-1900
  Data: 3G 1900, 3G 850

USB Modems

All prepaid devices (phones and modems) must be registered. To be registered, you need to have an El Salvadorian ID. We spent an agonizing hour at the Tigo headquarters trying to find a workaround. There was none. At Telcel in Mexico, a passport could be presented, and with a bit of patience you could manage to get things done. But this isn't Mexico. Tigo employees flat out refused to sell us anything unless we could present an El Salvadorian ID card.

From the Tigo store we headed to the roadside cheese shop, doubling as a Claro phone dealer. Turns out that Claro has the same deal, but the roadside shop was willing to offer the workaround. Pull out the registration papers from some other random dude, read off his name and ID number to the Claro agent, take the gringo's money, move along.

Lesson learned. When in El Salvador, don't go to the official store.

Our Claro USB modem cost $18, and came with 15 days of free data usage. Tigo modems cost more than $30, and included the same amount of free time. Coverage with the Claro modem was pretty good. The speed is hit or miss. In a big town with 3G it's excellent. When you get out in the woods, sometimes EDGE is your only option and downloads slow to a crawl.

Prepaid Phones

Prepaid phone SIM cards have the same restrictions as the modems. No El Sal ID, no SIM card. The trusty kiosk took care of our registration again and was extra helpful in explaining all those pesky details like how to check your balance and how to call internationally at discount rates.

All three phone companies in El Sal (Tigo, Movistar and Claro) offer packets (paquetes) for calling internationally. Claro had 30 minute packets for calling the USA for $0.75. They are easy to use: call a phone number, enter the code for the packet, and the cost is automatically deducted from your phone balance.

Related Articles

For more detailed information search LifeRemotely.com for the following related articles:

El Salvador Campgrounds and Hotels

El Salvador Wifi & Phone Report: More of the Same

El Salvador Budget Recap

The Passion of the Pork

El Salvador, Lesser of Two "Evils"

26

Honduras

Copan Ruins
Tegucigalapa
N

Quick Facts

Currency

Lempira

Exchange rate

19 lempiras = 1 US dollar

Cost of premium gas

$ 4.53/gallon

Note: We drove through Honduras in 3 hours, and other than a weekend trip to the Copan ruins from Antigua, we did not stop to visit any tourist attractions. We decided to skip most of this country because our CA-4 visas were very close to expiring and we preferred to spend the time in Nicaragua. We apologize for the lack of information in this section, but we didn't feel it was appropriate to write about a country we had so little first-hand knowledge of.

Driving & Roads

GPS & Paper Maps

Best paper map is from Reise Know How.
Open Street Maps and Cenrut.org are the best free GPS maps for Garmin.

Police & Military Checkpoints

In the 80-mile stretch between the El Salvador border and the Nicaragua border we passed 14 police checkpoint and were stopped at three of them.

Honduras requires you to carry two warning triangles, a fire extinguisher and a full-size spare tire. Police are notorious for stopping foreigners, asking for these things and not letting anyone get away without paying a bribe. We had our stuff in order, were polite to the officials and had no hassles. You could try the "I don't understand" route, but some of the officers spoke decent English and were obviously used to the "no entiendo" line.

Border Crossing

Paperwork Needed

- Passports
- Car title
- Car registration
- El Salvador vehicle permit and a copy
- 3 copies of the following: vehicle title, driver's passport photo page, driver's license, driver's passport page with Honduran stamp, driver's Honduran tourist card, reciept for the driver's tourist card, canceled El Salvador vehicle permit, vehicle registration, and finally the reciept for Honduran vehicle permit

Costs

For visas: $3 per person
For vehicles: $40 + $3.90 for copies

Two Borders in One Day

We crossed from San Miguel, El Salvador to Leon, Nicaragua in one day. This is the first of two border crossings we completed on Good Friday. A huge thanks to PanAmNotes.com for their guide on this crossing.

CA-4 Visas

Be aware that even though Honduras doesn't respect the CA-4, all other countries count your time in Guatemala, El Salvador, Honduras and Nicaragua cumulatively. You have 90 days total. No exceptions. Be prepared for steep fines if you overstay.

Crossing Into Honduras from El Salvador

Border name: El Amatillo
Closest major cities: Santa Rosa de Lima, El Salvador and San Andres, Honduras
Total time: 1 hour and 30 minutes
Date we crossed: April 6, 2012

Step by Step

1. At least a kilometer before the actual border crossing, stop at the white shack on the right, it's just after the speed bump. The official will cancel your El Salvador vehicle permit. Make sure you have a copy that he can stamp, you will need that later because he keeps the original.

2. Drive ahead about a kilometer. Take a left at the fork in the road, away from the new bridge.

3. Park on the right side of the immigration/customs building. Under the awning is fine, but try not to block traffic.

4. Go to the immigration counter and present your passports. The official will look over your passports and give you a small white piece of paper with the number of passports written on it. Keep the paper. Your passport will not be stamped (just as it wasn't stamped on entry).

5. Make copies of your canceled vehicle permit. You will need one to exit El Salvador and three on the Honduran side.

6. Get back in your car and drive to the start of the next bridge. An official will likely stop to collect your white slip of paper saying you went through immigration.
7. At the start of the bridge, another El Salvadorian official will collect a copy of your canceled El Salvadorian permit. Drive over the bridge.
8. Just over the bridge you will be stopped by a Honduran official. He will ask for your title and the passport and license of the person driving. If you have any doubt that this guy is an official, ask to see his ID.
9. He will instruct you where to park, about 150 meters ahead on the right at the aduana (customs) building.
10. The official will return the driver's passport and send you to immigration.
11. Walk over to immigration, pay a $3 per person entry fee and fill out your tourist card. Don't leave immigration without a passport stamp, a receipt and a tourist card.
12. Go to the copy shop. You will need three copies of: vehicle title, vehicle registration, driver's passport photo page, driver's license, driver's passport page with the new Honduran stamp, driver's tourist card, receipt for the tourist card and the canceled El Salvador vehicle permit.
13. Take your stack of copies back over to the aduana (customs) building. The official will take your pile of copies and spend a good bit of time entering it into a computer.
14. The official will add a vehicle import stamp to the driver's passport and then ask for a fee (around $40) and will present a receipt.

15. If it's Sunday or a holiday fees are paid in person, otherwise you will be directed to pay at a bank nearby.
16. You will need to go back to the copy shop and make three more copies of the receipt. The official will keep two copies. You will need the third copy when you leave the border area.
17. Make sure you have all of your original documents, and the numbers on the permits match the VIN and driver's IDs. Get back in your car and drive around the immigration building.
18. You may need to stop for fumigation here. We saw the white sign with green letters, but no one was around, and no one ever questioned us. We drove on.
19. In about a kilometer a guard will stop and ask to see a pile of paperwork. He will check the numbers and return everything except the copy of the permit receipt.
20. Drive away slowly, and be prepared for the plethora of police checkpoints between El Amatillo and the Nicaraguan border.

USB Modems & Cell Phones

Providers

- Digicel
- Claro
- Tigo

Frequencies

- Voice: GSM-850, 1900
- Data: 3G 1900

Related Articles

For more detailed information search LifeRemotely.com for the following related article:

A Weekend in Honduras

27

Nicaragua

Leon
Managua
Granada
Isla Ometepe
Playa Majagual
N

Quick Facts

Currency

Cordobas

Exchange rate

23 cordobas = 1 US dollar

Cost of premium gas

$5.47/gallon

Our per diem for 3 people

$70.99

Best local drink

Macuá (rum, lemon and guava juice)

Best street food

Gallo pinto

Best places to visit

Granada, Isla de Ometepe, Playa Majagual

Budget & Money

Currency:	Cordobas
Exchange rate to USD:	23 Cordobas = 1 US dollar
Are dollars accepted?	In tourist areas
Cost of premium gas:	$5.47/gallon
Miles driven:	667
Our per diem for 3 people:	$70.99

Per Diem Breakdown

Groceries	$255.60	22.26%
Lodging	$209.23	18.22%
Gas	$198.93	17.32%
Eating Out	$187.82	16.35%
Supplies	$74.87	6.52%
Transportation	$67.55	5.88%
Vehicle Import	$64.21	5.59%
Immigration	$54.63	4.76%
Entertainment and Tours	$42.08	3.66%
Coffee and Booze	$30.49	2.65%
Laundry	$15.00	1.31%
Gifts	$12.88	1.12%
Phone and Internet	$9.02	0.79%

Food & Accommodation Breakdown

Percent Time Camping	63%
Average Camping Cost	$5.17
Average Hotel Cost	$26.25
Daily Food Expenses	$25.51

Tips

- Not much new here. Camp, cook for yourself, research cheap hotels with kitchens ahead of time and save yourself some cash.
- Also, Joyita is stupid cheap Nicaraguan hooch that's not half bad. Just ask James over at HomeontheHighway.com.

Our Favorite Places

Granada

Granada is a beautiful colonial town. More touristy than Leon, but there is more to see and do and the city is much cleaner and easier to drive in. Feel free to enjoy some gringo delights such as a tasty can of Guinness at the Irish pub, but be prepared to pay more in areas that cater to tourists. Also, never pay for tours upfront, even when the operator offers you a "receipt" for your tickets.

Isla de Ometepe

You can take your vehicle out to Ometepe for about $25, plus passenger tickets. Ferries leave several times a day and you don't need to make a reservation if you're prepared to wait a couple hours. Stock up on food and booze in Rivas before you head to the island. There are no big grocery stores and food prices are high on Ometepe.

Playa Majagual

A few kilometers north of San Juan del Sur, this beach has it all. Super cheap camping ($5 per car), showers, bathrooms and a rogue unsecured wifi signal. Not to mention a gorgeous empty beach at your doorstep, and another around the corner that is perfect for watching sunsets.

Before you enter San Juan del Sur take the signed turn off to the north towards Playa Madera and Majagual. The road is dirt and not in excellent condition. Matilda's hostel offers rooms, but the campground next door is cheaper and has super-friendly owners.

Driving & Roads

GPS & Paper Maps

Best paper map is from Reise Know How.
Open Street Maps and Cenrut.org are the best free GPS maps for Garmin.

Road Conditions

In general the main highways are good. With one exception, there is a terrible stretch of the Pan-Am between Leon and Granada. The tar road is in bad shape and pothole dodging means you'll be driving 20 miles per hour the whole way. Smaller roads can be in great condition, but can also be terribly potholed with random patches of dirt at unforeseen intervals.

Roads on east side of Ometepe Island are good up until Balgue. The western roads are deteriorated, dirt and very bumpy.

Border Crossing

Paperwork Needed

- Passports
- Car title
- 3 copies of the driver's passport and license (2 for insurance, 1 for the permit)

Costs

Cost for visas: $12 USD per person
Cost for vehicle: $3 USD for fumigation. $12 USD for insurance.
Permit is free.

Skipping Honduras

It is possible to drive all the way from El Salvador to Leon, Nicaragua in one day, passing through Honduras in a few hours. We did it in about six hours. Be prepared to make lots of copies and test your patience. See our website for information on the El Salvador to Honduras crossing.

CA-4 Visas

Be aware that even though Honduras doesn't respect the CA-4, all other countries count your time in Guatemala, El Salvador, Honduras and Nicaragua cumulatively. You have 90 days total. No exceptions. We were reminded of this when we entered Nicaragua. And we have heard many horror stories of travelers being refused entry or forced to pay steep fines because they overstayed.

Insurance is Mandatory

Just because someone doesn't ask to see the paper, doesn't mean you don't need insurance. If someone doesn't approach you to sell it you'll have to hunt him or her down. Insurance is obligatory and the police will ask to see the paperwork at checkpoints.

Crossing Into Nicaragua from Honduras at Guasaule

Border name: Guasaule
Closest major cities: Guasaule, Honduras and Somotillo, Nicaragua
Total time: 1 hour
Date we crossed: April 20, 2012

Step by Step

1. When you see a small shack on the left of the road with a guard, go to the far left. It will look like a bomb recently went off in the area, and your intuition will be telling you that you are about to be mugged. Welcome to the Guasaule border.

2. The guard will ask to see your permit and they wave you forward. I repeat, stay to the LEFT. Drive all the way to the back, past the sketchy buildings. In the back of the parking lot you will see two gray buildings.

3. In the building to the left chances are the official will have moved his desk outside cause it's too damn hot. That's immigration. Give the hot grumpy dude your passport. Be nice, this has to be the worst border post on the planet.

4. He will stamp the passports and return them.

5. Wander aimlessly around the bombed-out wasteland looking for customs. Finally, walk to the back side of the building on the left, directly behind immigration.

6. There is no door, just a bunch of windows. A smiley lady will tell you through the barred window that she is a customs (aduana) official. Hand over your original Honduran vehicle permit and the driver's passport. She will keep the original permit and scribble on the stamp in the driver's passport, effectively canceling the permit.

7. Then with a smile, she'll wave you back to your car. Where you should go immediately, before the bombing starts again (ok, just kidding).

8. Drive back out of the parking lot, and head to Nicaragua.

9. When entering the border area, stay to the right. There will be a fumigation area. Roll up your windows and get fumigated.

10. Go to the window just after fumigation and pay the $3 fumigation fee. Keep the receipt.

11. At some point you will need to buy mandatory insurance. For us this happened at the fumigation shack. It cost $12, and you can buy it from anyone with a clipboard, providing they don't try to charge more than $12. She needs to see the driver's passport and title. She will ask for two copies of the drivers' IDs. Our insurance lady didn't keep the copies, she returned them with the vehicle paperwork.

12. From there, take a sharp left and park on the left side of the big parking lot. Look for the signs to migracion and aduana.

13. Go into the long building on the left of the parking lot (hidden behind all the trees). Immigration is in front of the building.

14. Hand over your passports, pay a $10 tourist card fee and a $2 tax per person. They do accept USD and have an ATM in the lobby that dispenses USD and Nicaraguan cordobas. Keep the receipt.

15. Head over to the aduana counter. Hand over your title, driver's passport and driver's license. The official will want a copy of the driver's documents but doesn't need a copy of the title.

16. The official will ask some random questions about the car and where you are going, then will issue a permit. Check the info on the permit carefully. Ours claimed that Kobus was from Sudan. Not far off from South Africa if you're in Nicaragua, I suppose. The official corrected without hassles.

17. With the vehicle permit, tourist card receipts, fumigation receipt and insurance paperwork in hand, drive to the right, past the immigration building.

18. Just past the building officers will stop and ask for all of the above paperwork and may verify your VIN. Then they'll send you on your way to Nicaragua.

19. Get to a hostel and have a mojito or six. Pass out. Do not repeat.

Internet & Wifi

General availability: Medium-high
Quality of bandwidth: Pretty terrible
Frequency of internet in campgrounds: Rare
Frequency of internet in hotels: Surprisingly high. Everywhere we stayed had internet access.

The Bottom Line

If you stick to the tourist route there will be plenty of wifi options, although the quality may be terrible. If you're heading out to a remote area, or just want to spend some time away from the crowds, pick up a USB modem before you go.

Connections

Same ol' story here. Free hostel wifi connections are painful at best. Connections die constantly, especially with frequent power outages.

Most hotels have free wifi. In remote areas, like Ometepe, there may be a fee. We saw more typical coffee and lunch cafés offering free wifi. Tourist places like Granada, Leon and San Juan del Sur have plenty of places to connect.

Like usual, if you need reliability, invest in a USB modem. If your work can wait and you have the patience, free wifi from hotels and cafés will work just fine.

USB Modems & Cell Phones

Costs

Prepaid modem: $25-33 USD
Prepaid SIM card: $2 USD
To call the USA per minute: $.19 USD

Providers

- Claro
- Movistar

Frequencies

- Voice: GSM-1900 and GSM-850
- Data: 3G 850

USB Modems

Claro modems are more expensive, 750 cordobas ($32.60 USD), but they come with an entire month of free time. Movistar modems are cheaper, about $25 USD, but they don't include any free time. Also, Movistar doesn't have any plans that last longer than a day, so you constantly have to activate new plans. This hassle made Claro a better choice for us.

The Claro modem had excellent coverage everywhere we went in Nicaragua, including the backwoods of Ometepe Island. Speeds were so good we could plug the dongle into our router and all three of us could work on the internet at once. Although $35 is steep for a modem, it was less than we would have spent frequenting internet cafés.

Prepaid Phones

While in Leon we purchased a prepaid SIM card. It was Easter weekend and the Claro shops were all closed, so we decided to go with Movistar this time. The SIM card cost C$50 ($2 USD) if you immediately recharged with another C$50 ($2 USD).

Like most Central American countries, recharges have promotional amounts that are usually double or triple your actual recharge. Unfortunately, with Movistar the promotional time is not available for international calls. It costs $.19 USD per minute to call the US or Canada. Some packets and promos are occasionally available, but given our short time in this country we decided not to bother to sort them out.

Related Articles

For more detailed information search LifeRemotely.com for the following related articles:

Nicaragua Campgrounds and Hotels

Nicaragua Budget Recap

Nicaragua Wifi & Phone Report

Campin', Nicaragua Style

Churches of León and Granada

Burnin' Up in Nicaragua

28

Costa Rica

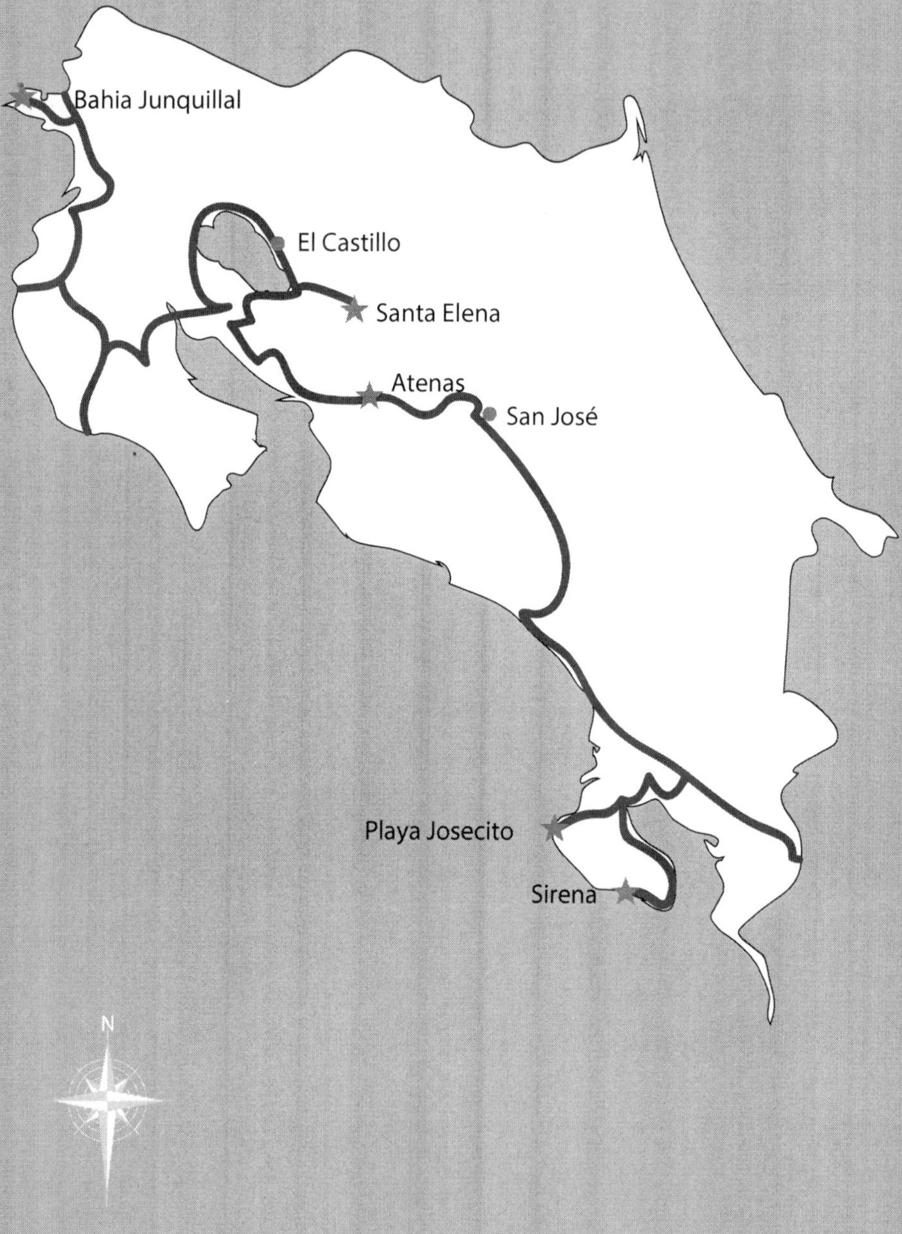
Bahia Junquillal
El Castillo
Santa Elena
Atenas
San José
Playa Josecito
Sirena
N

Quick Facts

Currency

Colones

Exchange rate

2500 colones = 1 US dollar

Cost of premium gas

$5.66/gallon

Our per diem for 3 people

$69.26

Best local drink

Cerveza michelada

Best street food

Ceviche

Best places to visit

Playa Josecito, Bahia Junquilla, Corcovado National Park

Budget & Money

Currency: Colones

Exchange rate to USD: 2500 colones = 1 US dollar

Are dollars accepted? In tourist areas

Cost of premium gas: $5.66

Miles driven: 983

Our per diem for 3 people: $69.26

Per Diem Breakdown

Groceries	$854.24	37.20%
Lodging	$451.18	19.65%
Gas	$404.89	17.63%
Eating Out	$160.57	6.99%
Park Fees	$144.16	6.28%
Entertainment & Tours	$98.29	4.28%
Supplies	$58.34	2.54%
Coffee & Booze	$41.02	1.79%
Laundry	$33.30	1.45%
Tolls & Parking	$21.26	0.93%
Phone & Internet	$20.06	0.87%
Gifts	$9.03	0.39%

Food & Accommodation Breakdown

Percent Time Camping	77.27%
Average Camping Cost	$14.34
Average Hotel Cost	$43.90
Daily Food Expenses	$28.19

Tips

- Stock up on supplies and basic food items in Nicaragua or Panama before crossing the border. No fruits, veggies or meat - just stuff like pasta, rice, canned goods, condiments, paper towels, tin foil, drinks etc. Food (and alcohol) prices are double in Costa Rica.
- Costa Rica is all about campin'. Bring your tent, bring your rain gear, bring your sleeping bag, enjoy some spectacular nature and save money.
- If you can sleep in your vehicle there are plenty of free places to stay. If you are tent camping, check out the beaches. Most are public land and are free to camp, ask the locals if it's safe and don't expect many facilities. Also, pack out your trash!
- Costa Rica is a great country to have friends and family come to visit. It's easy to get around, English is commonly spoken and if you're lucky you'll get to stay a week or two in a super-nice vacation home.
- Beware of the gringo isle in the supermarket. Costa Rican supermarkets are tempting because you can buy lots of stuff you haven't had in months, but on the other hand you're also going to pay way more than you would back home.

- Produce is expensive in supermarkets. Look for roadside stands to stock up on fruits and veggies. There aren't many small shops in Costa Rica, unlike other Central American countries, so shopping around is a good idea.
- Avoid eating at restaurants at all costs. Look for small places called "sodas" for some local flavor (rice, beans and meat), but still expect to pay at least $5 a plate.

Our Favorite Places

Bahia Junquilla

Bahia Junquilla is situated just north of Santa Rosa National park, very close to the Nicaraguan border. The entry fee is a steep $13 per person, so plan to stay a few days to make the fee worth it. The campground was the best-maintained site we'd seen since the US. The park rangers are very friendly and can tell you where and when to find wildlife, including monkeys and a huge variety of birds. The beach and surrounding wildlife preserve is incredible. We saw more critters on our first day than we saw in two weeks in Nicaragua.

Playa Josecito

This pristine beach is located south of Bahia Drake on an unnamed and unmarked road that will likely not be on your GPS. The beach is absolutely beautiful and scarlet macaws are everywhere. There is nothing here but a small school, a soccer field and a house. You can camp on the beach, or on the lawn in from of the house. We were told the field floods and the beach washes out often, so the grass in front of the house is your best bet.

There is a freshwater shower (hose) near the beach and the owners at the house can give you a key to use the bathroom at the school. There is a restaurant and lodge ten minutes walk north on the beach called Poor Man's Paradise. If you want to camp out with the scarlet macaws and get a taste of Corcovado without entering the park this is a great place to go.

A 4x4 is highly recommended because there are rivers to cross, but nothing worse than you would have crossed getting to Bahia Drake. Check road conditions before you leave, the road may be impassible if it has rained heavily.

Corcovado National Park

It's been called the most biologically intense place on earth. Unfortunately (or maybe fortunately) it remains a difficult place to get to. Either pay a pretty penny for a boat ride from Bahia Drake or Puerto Jimenez, or hike there from Carate or one of the other ranger stations on the western side of the peninsula. One does not simply drive to Corcovado National Park.

Puerto Jiminez is the place to stay before your trip. You must arrange your park pass and sleeping reservations at the office in town before setting out. The dirt road to Carate isn't in great shape and may be impassable after heavy rain. A 4x4 is required, you will be getting wet. At Carate you can camp for free on the beach and you can park near the shop for $5 per day while you venture into the jungle. From Carate it's an amazing 12-mile hike to the Sirena ranger station. It's hot, full of mosquitoes, and you have to time the tides right or you'll end up stranded. Plan ahead.

The ranger station in Sirena has dorm beds, worth the $8 per person so you don't have to pack in a tent. Camping is $5 per person. The meals at Sirena are ridiculously expensive $20-$25 per person per meal. We recommend you pack in a stove and easy-to-cook meals. Plan on staying at least two nights in Sirena to recover from the hike in and to explore the area around the ranger station. The wildlife here is incredible. There is no other place like this on Earth. Without a doubt, it's worth the trip.

Driving & Roads

GPS & Paper Maps

Best paper map is from Reise Know How.
Open Street Maps and Cenrut.org are the best free GPS maps for Garmin.

Road Conditions

It's a mixed bag in Costa Rica. Main highways are usually in good condition, especially around San Jose. Outside the cities conditions can deteriorate quickly. There are some new toll roads around San Jose, especially near the airport, but the fees aren't much compared to Mexico.

Dirt roads are common in Costa Rica around eco-tourist areas. Driving to Monte Verde, Arenal and Corcovado all involve a bit of dirt and dust. Roads are generally in decent shape but can deteriorate rapidly depending on traffic and rainfall. Guidebooks will tell you what to expect, but asking someone before you head out is the best way to find out about current conditions.

The Rainy Season

The rainy season in Costa Rica starts in May and lasts through August. Afternoon thunderstorms are common and happen nearly every day in many parts of the country. The closer you get to July and August, the worse the rains will be. A day or two of heavy rain will turn creeks into rivers which can leave you stranded on the wrong side of the road.

The Road to Monte Verde

No matter which way you go to the cloud forests of Santa Elena and Monte Verde you will be forced to drive on a long dirt road. It's not nearly as bad (in the dry season) as the guidebooks say, just be careful around turns because trucks and busses like to take up both lanes. One more than on occasion we were nearly pushed off the road.

The Road from Volcan Arenal to Monte Verde

If you are traveling south from Arenal to Monte Verde there is a beautiful back road connecting the two attractions. It's not on many maps, but it's a fantastic 4x4 route and can cut several hours off your trip.

In El Castillo you can camp on Lake Arenal for free. There are no facilities, but it's a beautiful spot. From there, continue on the road through El Castillo, heading west along the south end of the lake. You'll come to a river crossing just outside town. We crossed in May, just at the start of the rainy season when the river was a bit higher than normal.

After the river crossing it's another hour and a half on a scenic dirt road until you connect with the main road heading south to Santa Elena and Monte Verde. We wouldn't recommend doing this route in reverse unless you know the condition of the river crossing.

Border Crossing

Paperwork Needed

- Passports
- Car title
- 1 copy of the vehicle title and mandatory Costa Rican insurance
- 1 copy of the passport photo page, driver's license and immigration entry stamp for each person who intends to drive the car in Costa Rica.

Costs

For visas: $67 cordobas ($3 USD) per person
($1 USD tax and $2 USD for the stamp)
For vehicles: $2,175 colones ($4.50 USD) fumigation,
$8,365 colones ($17 USD) insurance

Crossing Into Costa Rica from Nicaragua

Border name: Peñas Blancas
Closest major cities: San Juan del Sur, Nicaragua and La Cruz, Costa Rica
Total time: 2 hours
Date crossed: Saturday, April 23, 2012

Step by Step

1. Stop at the small booth on the left side of the road. If it's busy, park just past the booth.

2. Give your passports to one of the guards out front. They will look at them, but not do anything.
3. Give the vehicle permit to another man near the booth, he will scribble something on it and hand it back.
4. Get back in the car and drive a short distance. Go past the set of buildings ahead and turn left. Then drive past the customs/immigration building and turn left again. Park here.
5. Walk around the other side of the building to the exit immigration. At the small booth pay the $1 per person exit tax.
6. Proceed to the immigration window. Fill out your tourist exit card. Pay a $2 fee to the official and he will issue a receipt. Keep all receipts!
7. Head back to the other side of the building and find an official in a while shirt with the DGA Logo. Hand over your Nicaraguan vehicle permit. He may want to check your car and/or verify the VIN. He will then stamp/sign/scribble on your permit.
8. The next step is to find a police officer, possibly in the building, possibly wandering around outside. The officer will add another signature and stamp to your permit. He may also inspect the car.
9. Proceed to the small window on the corner of the building. Here another official with a DGA polo shirt will take your permit again. She will enter a few things in the computer and hand your uber-stamped-up permit back to you.
10. Get back in your car and haul it to Costa Rica before they ask for more stamps.

11. When leaving the border area, an official at a small shack will ask to see all the passports and the vehicle permit. He will keep your uber-stamped-up import permit.
12. Stay to the right and stop at the fumigation booth. Pay the CR$2175 fee, and then proceed through the fumigation station. Note that cordobas, colones and US dollars are accepted here.
13. Continue to the big white immigration building on the left. Just past it, also on the left, is a good place to park.
14. Go to immigration, fill out your entry cards and present the card with your passports to the official. Your passport will be stamped and returned. Now for the fun part.
15. Look across the street at the small yellow building that says “aduana” on front. I know you want to go there. But don’t be fooled. This is not the aduana you are looking for (at least not yet). Get back in your car and drive about 300 meters to the “other” aduana or walk if you can stand the heat.
16. Go to the insurance window on the side at the far end of the building. Hand over the vehicle title, the driver’s passport and license. Pay the fee, $8365 colones ($17 USD)
17. Go to the copy shop. Make sure you have one copy of the title and insurance paper. You will also need one copy of the passport photo page, immigration stamp, and driver’s license for every person that intends to drive the vehicle in Costa Rica.
18. Get back in your car and drive back to the first aduana booth. The official here will take all of your copies and originals. He’ll ask you to fill out a form, and return your original and your copies with the form on top all neatly stapled together. He may verify your VIN and search your car.

19. With the paperwork you have from aduana #1, drive back to aduana #2. Go through the doors at the very end of the building. Hand over the pile of paperwork you received at aduana #1. Enjoy the air conditioning.
20. The official will enter more info into the computer and hand back a new piece of paper, this is your vehicle import permit.
21. Stop at the small exit booth and show your vehicle permit to the guard. Get out of Dodge.

Internet & Wifi

General availability: High
Quality of bandwidth: Medium-high
Frequency of internet in campgrounds: Rare, most campgrounds are in national reserves. Don't expect any internet unless there is a hotel or restaurant nearby.
Frequency of internet in hotels: High (we think). We only stayed at two hotels and both had internet.

The Bottom Line

Hotels and hostels have excellent internet, you can rely on it as long as you can handle the occasional power or network outage. If you're going into the wild and need to stay connected, bring an unlocked 3G modem with you and pick up a SIM card at a nearby shop.

Connections

Costa Rica is the most expensive and economically stable of all Central American countries, internet here is plentiful. Cafés are everywhere in town, but be prepared to pay a premium in tourist areas.

Connection speeds are usually excellent. Just expect random network and power outages to interrupt service periodically.

If you're planning to camp in national parks or reserves, don't count on having internet or cell phone signal. Quite a few places we went (Bahia Junquillal, Bahia Drake in Osa, and the highlands south of San Jose) did not have cell phone reception. Usually we could drive 5 or 10 miles back up the road and find a signal strong enough to get things done.

If you need reliable connections, invest in a 3G modem and SIM cards from more than one company.

The Monopoly Ends

As part of the requirements for the Central American Free Trade Agreement, Costa Rica was required to privatize their nationally run cell phone service in late 2011. The former monopoly, run by Grupo ICE, was spilt into three new companies; Claro, Movistar and Kolbi. You'll recognize Claro and Movistar as big players in the industry throughout other countries in the Americas. Kolbi is the privatized version of the former Grupo ICE.

Kindles Don't Work

For one reason or another, kindles with free 3G do not work in Costa Rica. It could be because of the recent split of the government companies, it could be because Costa Rica only runs 3G on the less-common 850 frequency. Either way, we tried it repeatedly without success.

The Strange Frequency

Costa Rica uses GSM-1800 for voice and 850 for 3G. GSM-1800 is a common frequency for those coming from Europe, Asia or Australia, but it's not normal for the Americas, especially the US. Almost all quad-band phones will support this frequency, but tri-band phones may not.

If you already have a phone and modem that have been working throughout Central America, and for some reason they stop working in Costa Rica, the lack of GSM-1800 or 3G-850 frequency support is your problem.

Note that some 3G-2100 frequency rights have been issued. But that won't help if you're trying to make voice calls.

USB Modems & Cell Phones

Costs

Prepaid modem: Not for sale. Unlocked modem plus SIM card ~$70 USD
Prepaid SIM card: $5 USD
To call the USA per minute: $.26 USD

Providers

- Kolbi: Grupo ICE
- Movistar
- Claro

Frequencies

- Voice: GSM-1800
- Data: 3G 850 and 2100

USB Modems

No Prepaid Modems for Sale

Normally in Central America we were able to show up at any moderately-sized cell phone shop and buy a prepaid USB modem without hassle. Most prepaid modems come with a month of free airtime, so it was never worth the hassle of trying to buy a SIM card and set up our unlocked modem. Costa Rica changed that.

In more than a dozen phone stores run by Claro, Movistar and Kolbi that we visited, we could not find a prepaid modem. After consulting with our overlanding friends we discovered that some stores sold modems on a contract basis, and others required a Costa Rican ID. Unless you can talk a Tico into buying one for you, you're out of luck.

You can buy an unlocked USB modem, and most shops will offer to set it up for you. Prices are steep though, around $70. If you brought an unlocked modem with you that supports the 3G-850 frequency, then you've survived half the battle.

Setting Up an Unlocked Modem

Costa Rica quickly became a crash course in understanding how USB modems work. It doesn't take too much effort, provided that you have the right hardware and network codes. We found that it's totally useless to go into a store and expect help with this setup. Occasionally you'll find a brilliant employee, but most staff will shrug, refuse to issue a refund and ignore you until you go away.

Step 1: Buy a SIM card. Put some money on the SIM card. A dollar or two to start is safe until you are sure it will work. We have only tested this with Kolbi and Movistar, so we can only recommend those two providers. But there's no reason why Claro wouldn't work as well.

Step 2: Activate the SIM. Most places you buy the card from will do this for you. If not, ask them to. It usually involves putting the SIM in a phone and dialing a few numbers.

Step 3: Put the PIN number for your SIM in a safe place. You will need this number.

Step 4: Put the SIM card in your USB dongle and plug that into your computer.

Step 5: Set up a new connection profile settings for your modem. Most modems come with a predefined list of connection profiles, but because Costa Rican companies are relatively new, most modems do not include their network profiles. You will need to setup a new profile and enter the APN. For Kolbi the APN is "kolbi3g" for Movistar it is "internet.movistar.cr". A quick Google search will give you the correct profiles for any company in the world.

Step 6: Set your new profile as default, if your software requires this step.

Step 7: Use the text message software that came with your modem to sign up for an internet package. With Kolbi you send a text to 6060 that says either "dia" or "semana". One day costs 200 colones (roughly $.40 USD). With Movistar send a text to 606 that says either hora, dia or semana. Movistar is slightly more expensive, but the one hour option is helpful if you need to do something quick.

Step 8: Wait for a confirmation message that your package has been activated.

Note that with Kolbi, you can skip steps 7 and 8, connect directly, and pay per kilobyte. This will work fine for quick browsing, but if you plan to use a lot of data, it's more cost effective to sign up for a full day plan.

Step 9: Hit the "connect" button and surf away.

Checking your balance: To check your balance with Kolbi send a blank text message to 1150. To check your balance with Movistar send a message to 606 with the word "saldo" in the body. Saldo means balance in Spanish.

Recharging: As usual, stop by any roadside shop and give them your phone number and the amount you want to recharge. They'll send some magic numbers via their phone and you'll get a text confirming your recharge. Most companies also sell prepaid cards in increments of 1000 colones. You can buy a card, scratch off the pin number and call to recharge. There is an option to do this in English. If you buy cards to recharge you'll have to use your phone, there's no way to do this from a modem.

Prepaid Phones

Costa Rica is the most expensive country in Central America for calling the US. On average companies charge $0.26 per minute to call the US, compared to $0.13 a minute in Panama. It might be a good idea to look into VOIP options.

Related Articles

For more detailed information search LifeRemotely.com for the following related articles:

Costa Rica Campgrounds and Hotels

Costa Rica Phone & Wifi Report: Unlocked Dongles for the Win

Costa Rica Budget Recap

Corcovado National Park

Pura Vida

Costa Rica: Central America Lite or Overlanding Playground?

Campin' With Critters in Costa Rica

29

Panama

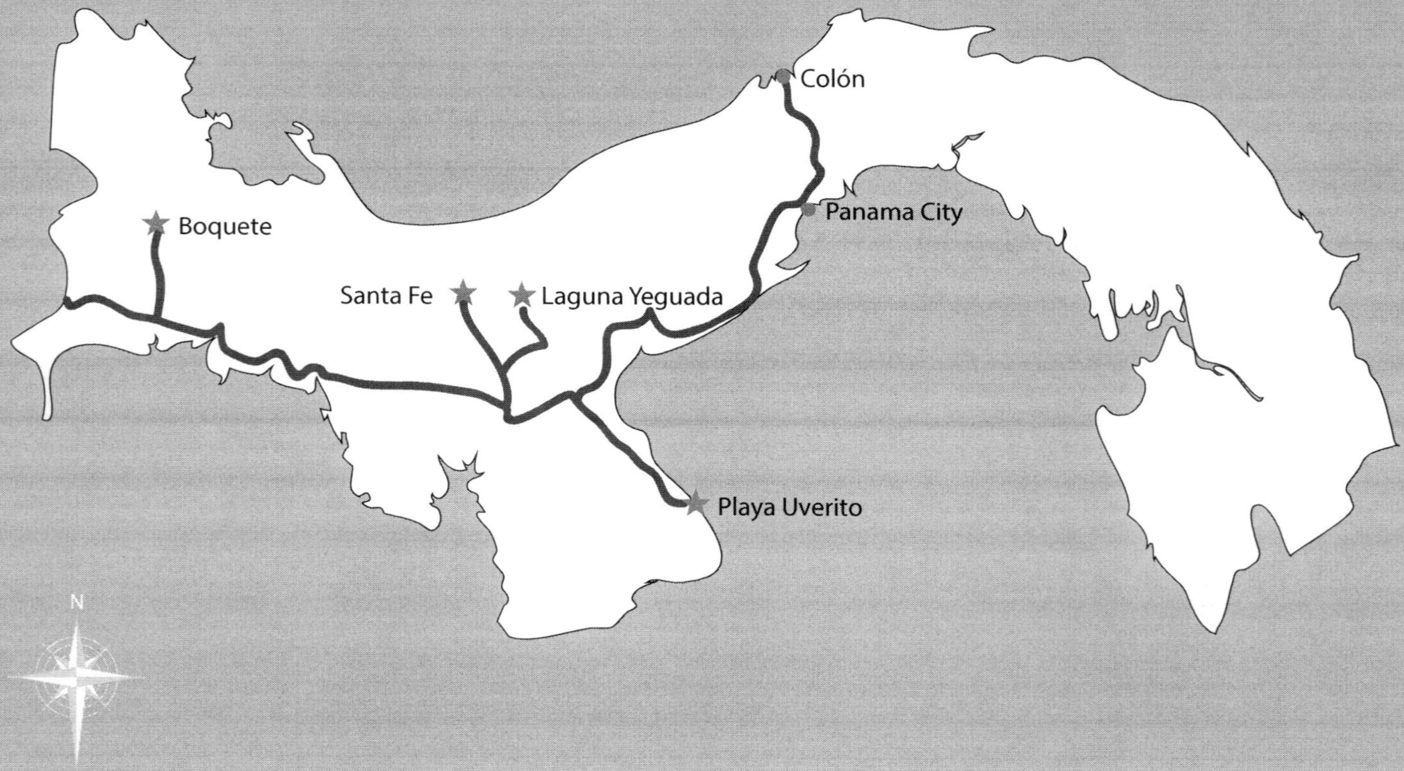
Colón
Panama City
Boquete
Santa Fe
Laguna Yeguada
Playa Uverito
N

Quick Facts

Currency

Balboas

Exchange rate

1 balboa = 1 US dollar (fixed)

Cost of premium gas

$4.40/gallon

Our per diem for 3 people

$94.02

Best local drink

Balboa cerveza

Best street food

Spiral-cut chorizo on a stick

Best places to visit

Boquete, Laguna Yeguada, San Blas Islands, Panama Canal

Budget & Money

Currency:	Balboas
Exchange rate to USD:	1 balboa = 1 US dollar (fixed)
Are dollars accepted?	Yep, the currency is the same except for $.50 and $1 coins.
Cost of premium gas:	$4.40 per gallon
Miles driven:	1091
Our per diem for 3 people:	$94.02

Per Diem Breakdown

Lodging	$624.84	37.20%
Groceries	$314.87	18.75%
Gas	$278.25	16.57%
Supplies	$158.23	9.42%
Eating Out	$119.00	7.08%
Entertainment & Tours	$75.00	4.47%
Transportation	$32.00	1.91%
Border Fees	$31.53	1.88%
Tolls & Parking	$10.00	0.63%
Phone & Internet	$10.00	0.63%

Food & Accommodation Breakdown

Percent Time Camping	31.58%
Average Camping Cost	$15.33
Average Hotel Cost	$44.60
Daily Food Expenses	$22.84

One-Time Expenses

Dairen Gap Shipping costs:

$1050 to for half of a shared 40' container
$1055 for three one-way flights to Cartagena

Note: We paid an additional $500 in fees on the Colombian side, shared with our shipping partners.

Tips

- Food in Panama, even imported food from the US, is cheaper than Costa Rica. Panama's a great place to enjoy a taste of home, and the variety of international restaurants in the city makes it a fantastic place to grab a bite of something you've been missing.
- Driving in Panama City is a stressful experience and parking is hard to find. Fortunately, taxis are everywhere and it usually costs less than $5 to get to where you need to go within the central districts.
- Finding a budget hotel in Panama City with secured parking is difficult. Looking online and calling ahead is a safe bet to avoid having to drive around the city in search of a cheap place to spend a few nights. Don't rely on what the website or guidebook says, it was wrong for us.

- If you want to stay put for a while, Panama's a great place to find a budget rental house for a week. Ours had two bedrooms, AC, (bad) internet, and a fully stocked kitchen for less than we paid for an average hotel room.
- Plan an extra couple hundred dollars to deal with getting your car to South America on top of the shipping fees. Taxis, hotels, and being forced to eat out will add to your per diems over the course of the 4-5 days it takes to deal with the process.
- Likewise, don't budget for the cheapest available flights (assuming you're flying) to get from Panama City to South America. Due to the uncertainty of the entire process, you will be forced to book flights last minute which usually costs more.
- Research recent costs for shipping your car to South America. The numbers we originally found were three years old, and prices have nearly doubled since then.
- Taking the train from Colon back to Panama City after dropping off your car is a great way to see the canal, just be aware it costs $25 per person.

Our Favorite Places

Boquete

About 2 hours from the Costa Rica border, Boquete is a small town up in the mountains. Coming from the sweltering coast of Costa Rica the cool mountain air here was a welcome break. There are lots of coffee tours and hikes to do, or just sit around and enjoy the nice people and charming town.

Laguna Yeguada

East of Boquete, up in the mountains, lies a lake called Yeguada. It's inside a park and unfortunately has a steep entry fee. But the camping and the views are excellent. There's fishing and hiking and plenty to keep you relaxed, just don't expect much in the way of facilities.

San Blas Islands

We didn't visit the San Blas islands, but it's certainly on our list to return to. Although the sailing trips get mixed reviews, usually depending on the weather, the islands are undoubtedly worth a visit.

Panama Canal

No doubt that you will end up seeing at least some part of the Panama Canal. Despite the hassle of trying to deal with shipping your car and getting to Colombia, taking the time to tour the canal is recommended. Short on time, we took the train ride back from Colon to Panama City. It's a beautiful ride, well worth the $25 ticket cost.

Driving & Roads

GPS & Paper Maps

Best paper map is from Reise Know How.
Open Street Maps and Cenrut.org are the best free GPS maps for Garmin.

Road Conditions

The roads in Panama are surprisingly good. Well-maintained four-lane highways are common. There are motorcycle police everywhere. You will often find them parked in the opposite lane, but they are checking your speed…sneaky like that.

Police & Military Checkpoints

There is a checkpoint just across the border where you will need to show the vehicle paperwork and passports for all passengers. Throughout the rest of the country checkpoints are rare.

Border Crossing

Paperwork Needed

- Passports
- Car title
- 2 copies of the driver's passport, driver's license and the vehicle title (one copy is for aduana, the other for insurance)

Costs

For visas: $1 per person for Panama entry
For vehicles: $15 for insurance, $1.60 for copies

Changing Money

If you need to change money, do it at the BCR bank in no man's land before you get to Panama. No other banks around will change colones.

Double Check Your Permit

If you plan to ship your car to Colombia, triple check that EVERYTHING on your permit is correct. Especially that your VIN number is listed for both your chassis and engine number, and that your vehicle type is correct.

Crossing Into Panama from Costa Rica

Border Name: Paso Canoas
Closest Major Cities: Ciudad Neily, Costa Rica and David, Panama
Total Time: 1 hour 15 minutes
Date Crossed: Monday May 28, 2012

Step by Step

1. Park next to the Costa Rican immigration office. It's on the left side of the road when driving towards Panama.

2. Go to the salida window, fill out your exit card and hand over the exit form with your passport. The official will stamp and return your passport.

3. Go around the back of the immigration building to the aduana office.

4. Explain that you want to cancel your temporary vehicle permit and you will be given a simple form to fill out.

5. Fill out the form and hand it to the official along with the original permit papers and the driver's passport. He or she will want to go to your car to verify the VIN number.

6. Back at the office, the official will cancel the permit, keep the original, and return the form you filled out with a stamp on it. This is your proof of cancellation.

7. Get back in your car and drive to the Panama side.

8. Drive under the right side of the dirty white open-air building. You can park next to the curb on the left.

9. Go to the farthest end of the building and you will see the windows for immigration entrada. If the line is short, go here first.

10. Someone will approach you and ask for your passports, he or she will put a small sticker on a page in your passport. The cost is $1 per sticker. You can pay in colones but the exchange rate is not good.

11. Give the official behind the window your passports. She/he will type in some stuff, take your photo, and stamp and return the passports.

12. Next, walk across the street to the insurance office. Hand over the vehicle title and driver's passport, a copy of both and $15. You'll be issued two identical pieces of paper. One will be kept by the aduana, the other is for you.

13. Go back across the street and up the stairs to the transito office. Hand over your insurance paperwork and the driver's passport. They will stamp and return the insurance papers.

14. Go back down stairs to the aduana window. The sign on the window reads "Captura y Manifesto". You should see a piece of paper taped to the window that says "Turismo", that's the right line.

15. The official will need your title, driver's passport, a copy of both, and the two insurance papers. The official will enter a bunch of stuff in the computer and will return originals and one copy of the insurance. They will also issue you a vehicle import permit.

16. Take your new permit to the random official guy with a clipboard who loiters outside the aduana window. Don't worry, he'll probably find you. He'll inspect your car and verify the VIN number. He will also stamp your permit.

17. Head out of the border area, make sure to drive through the fumigation area.

18. In about 1 km you will be stopped at a military post and will have to show your permit, insurance and passports for everyone in the car.

19. That's all. Enjoy the four-lane highway and cheap beer.

Internet & Wifi

General availability: High
Quality of bandwidth: Medium
Frequency of internet in campgrounds: Average. Camping in a hostel or hotel, there will be internet. Camping at a national park, not a chance.
Frequency of internet in hotels: High

The Bottom Line

Internet in hotels and internet cafés is your best bet. Don't count on it in restaurants or café, except in some areas of Panama City. If you need reliability, get a 3G USB modem and stick to the beaten path.

Connections

In general, internet is available everywhere. There were small internet cafés in every town, and several in tourist areas. Some restaurants and coffee shops had internet, but not as many as you'd think. Surprisingly, in the town of Boquete which is known for its huge selection of coffee shops, we drove around for more than an hour looking for one that had internet without luck.

We only camped at two places in Panama: Boquete and near Laguna Yeguada. The place we stayed in Boquete was a hostel and had wifi in the common area. Laguana Yeguada is a protected park and the list of amenities started and ended with a pit toilet.

Quality of Bandwidth

As usual, bandwidth quality was all over the place. The house we rented in Playa Uverito (near Las Tablas) had painfully slow and unreliable internet.

Our hotel in Panama City had shockingly fast internet which worked about half of the time we were there.

Like the rest of Central America, don't count on fast anything. Panama is better than most other countries, but not without issues. If you need reliable connections pick up a 3G USB modem.

USB Modems & Cell Phones

Costs

Prepaid modem: $37.50 with Claro
Prepaid SIM card: $5.00
To call the USA per minute: $0.13

Providers

- Cable & Wireless aka Mas Movil
- Claro
- Digicel
- Movistar

Frequencies

- Voice: GSM-850 and GSM-1900

USB Modems

There are several options for setting up a USB modem in Panama. Claro sells a prepaid modem for $37.50, and we don't think it comes with any free time. Prepaid packets range between $1 per day and $15 per month.

We attempted to buy a Claro SIM and install it in our unlocked modem. Even with the right APN, the card only worked for a few minutes. Our modem may have been blocked, but we don't know for certain.

Cable & Wireless (branded as Mas Movil) did not offer prepaid modems, but they did let us buy a SIM and said it would work in our unlocked modem. The employees at the store were very helpful and offered to set it up for us. They also said that if it didn't work they would refund the cost of the SIM.

We put the SIM in our phone and signed up for a one day data package (call *465# and follow the prompts). After signing up for the data package we put the SIM into our unlocked modem and plugged it into a laptop. We setup a new connection profile using the APN we found online using our phone. (See the Costa Rica Phone and Wifi Report for how to set this up.)

The Cable & Wireless setup worked fine. The connection speeds weren't great, and out at Playa Uverito the signal was terrible. A lot of the time we were on EDGE or slower networks. Moving the SIM to the phone every time we wanted to sign up for another day was also a pain. But it was substantially cheaper than buying a Claro modem.

Movistar and Digicel also operate in Panama, but we found that the offices in David do not sell prepaid modems. Digicel does advertise on their site that you can setup an unlocked modem by installing a prepaid SIM.

Prepaid Phones

Cost for a SIM card is about $5, but it usually includes $5 of free time. Cable & Wireless (aka Mas Movil) told us the cost to call the US was $.04 per minute. It sounded too good to be true, and it was. The actual cost is $.04 per minute international surcharge on top of the regular $.09 per minute to make regular calls. Claro and Movistar have similar rates, $.12-$.14 per minute.

The week before we left Panama we discovered an international packet that cost $2.00 for 60 minutes of phone time to call the US. With Cable & Wireless call *123# and follow the prompts. This type of packet is common throughout Central America, but is often not advertised. Check your provider's website, and watch for the promo text messages on your phone, this is how we found out about it.

Related Articles

For more detailed information search LifeRemotely.com for the following related articles:

Shipping Across the Darien Gap: Panama to Colombia Part 1

Panama Budget Recap

Panama Phone & Wifi Report: Good but not Great

Panama: Mountains, Vetkoek and Dirty-Dancing Devils

Conclusion

We've attempted to supply a breath of information about overlanding in Mexico and Central America, along with advice and information from others. But feel free to ignore much of it. It's hard to call this trip an adventure if you're simply following someone else's path.

Plenty of overlanders start this trip with little more than the plan to drive south until the money runs out. Others, like us, spend hours researching and planning. This book is largely a result of that choice.

If you found this book useful, we encourage you to share it with others. Our goal is to help as many people as possible to realize the dream of traveling the Americas by car. It's a journey unlike any other, and one that will permanently change how you look at the world.

Stay in Touch

Visit our website: **www.LifeRemotely.com**

Like us on Facebook:
www.facebook.com/LifeRemotely

Follow us on Twitter:
https://twitter.com/LifeRemotely

Questions, comments or corrections? Email us at info@liferemotely.com.

Resources

Overlanding Friends

Special thanks to these guys for providing us information, allowing us to use some of their content, and generally being awesome people:

Drive Nacho Drive – (www.drivenachodrive.com) Brad and Sheena are driving their 1984 Vanagon, named Nacho, from their home in Arizona to South America and beyond. What Brad lacks in fishing skills he more than makes up for as an emergency roadside VW mechanic.

PanAm Notes – (www.panamnotes.com) Brianna and Logan completed their 449-day, 22,000-mile journey in March 2012. Along with a blog of their trip, their website contains a wealth of information for overlanders.

Home on the Highway – (www.homeonthehighway.com) We've shared more than one bottle of cheap Central American hooch with James and Lauren. Driving their trusty first generation Toyota 4Runner from California to Argentina, they have few plans but to head south until the road runs out.

Anywhere That's Wild – (www.anywherethatswild.org) Jill and Zach are driving an amazing 2003 AWD Astro Van from their home in Massachusetts. Their goal is to discover the beauty of the natural world and its many cultures.

Joydrive – (www.joydrive.ca) Kelsey and Tom completed their trip in December 2009 driving a '91 Volkswagen Golf over 31,000 miles.

The Darien Plan – (www.thedarienplan.com) Kristin and Chris spent 16 months driving from their home in California to Argentina. Along with Kelsey and Tom of Joydrive, Kristen and Chris are cofounders of Drive The Americas, one of the best resources for overlanding in North and South America.

Capitol Southbound – (www.capitolsouthbound.com) We met Cesar and Danni in Panama City. They're driving a second generation Toyota 4Runner with a rooftop tent and hope to reach Argentina in early 2013.

Ruined Adventures – (www.ruinedadventures.com) Brenton and Shannon hit the road in early 2012 in their first generation 4Runner. The plan? Drive down the Americas, up Africa and everywhere in between.

Along the way we've met and been in contact with many fellow overlanders. Read more about their journeys here:

Head South – (www.headsouth.travellerspoint.com) Paul and Susie drove from their home in Canada to Alaska and then to Costa Rica. They're currently fighting fires in Canada, but they will be back on the road soon, hopefully in time to share a few more beers with us in South America.

Adventure The Americas – (www.adventuretheamericas.com) We met this crazy trio in Costa Rica after they spotted our 4Runner in a hotel parking lot. Their plan is to drive from Colorado to Argentina and back, around both coasts of South America, in six months.

Earthcircuit – (www.earthcircuit.org) We ran into Andy, Dunia, with their dog Vaga and retired wheelchair bus Jigsaw in Panama. They left home in England in 2010 and drove across Europe and Asia before heading into North and Central America.

...Por America Adando – (www.poramericaandando.blogspot.com) We met this Argentinian couple in Panama. Joaquin and Clara are headed the opposite direction, hoping to reach Alaska in 2013.

Seventeen by Six – (www.seventeenbysix.wordpress.com) Jeremy and Paula left London in 2012 to slowly travel the world in a 1997 VW Eurovan they bought in California.

Trans-Americas Journey – (www.trans-americas.com) Eric and Karen quit their jobs to travel the Americas in 2008. So far they've visited ten countries with the goal of hitting all 23 in the Western Hemisphere.

Outside of the Box – (www.rumziehen.blogspot.com) Tine and Matthias are cycling around the Americas. These two are hardcore!

Global Road Trekker - (www.globalroadtrekker.com) Jim and Wendy are redefining their American Dream with a three-year road trip adventure around the world. We wish they would hurry and catch up!

From A to B – (www.fromatob.org) Mark and Sarah quit their jobs in London to travel the Americas by truck starting June 2011.

Overlanding Resources

WikiOverland – (www.wikioverland.org) A quickly expanding wiki site full over overland info for everywhere in the world. Easy to update with your own information. Managed by Dan of TheRoadChoseMe.com, who completed the Pan-America drive in his Jeep not too long ago.

Drive The Americas – (www.drivetheamericas.com) This website provided us the "AH HAH!" moment when we first started planning our trip. It can be done! Along with being the best resource for driving through North and South America, it contains a huge list of other road trippers. Contact Kristin to have your profile added, it's one of the best ways to meet up with other overlanders traveling online.

Expedition Portal – (www.expeditionportal.com) A fantastic resource for overlanders heading in every direction. Read about in progress and completed adventures in the forums.

Printed in Poland
by Amazon Fulfillment
Poland Sp. z o.o., Wrocław

27629503R00201